JEFFREY MICHAEL SMITH

To: Jane

Love, Bill

2023

ON YOUR SIDE TODAY

How to Know God is Truly Good

LONGSPAN BOOKS
Louisville, Kentucky

JEFFREY MICHAEL SMITH

ON YOUR SIDE TODAY

How to Know God is Truly Good

Unless otherwise noted, all Scripture quotations are
taken from the Christian Standard Bible®, Copyright ©
2017 by Holman Bible Publishers. Used by permission.
Christian Standard Bible® and CSB® are federally
registered trademarks of Holman Bible Publishers.

Scripture quotations marked ESV are from the ESV®
Bible (The Holy Bible, English Standard Version®),
Copyright © 2016 by Crossway, a publishing ministry
of Good News Publishers. Used by permission.
All rights reserved.

ISBN 979-8-9868520-0-3 (paperback)

Longspan Books (Louisville, KY)
longspanbooks.com

To my God, who holds close
Ann Gayle Bennett Smith (1970-2002)
and
Richard Michael Smith (1945-1993)
along with all those
who trust the good news

CONTENTS

CONTENTS

PREFACE

Imagine that during the next few minutes you have an extraordinary encounter with God. Everything else around you becomes dim. Your thoughts become incredibly clear. All your problems, large and small, are momentarily forgotten. And as improbable as it may seem, you sense that the God of the universe is trying to come close, break through your thoughts, and speak to you.

So you listen.

And in that moment, to your great amazement, you feel an outpouring of love from God that's hard to describe. You realize God wants to be close to you. You aren't afraid of him or fearful of what he might do. You feel that he wants the best for you—even greater than you can imagine. You sense that his feelings toward you are benevolent and pure. In that moment, you find yourself believing God is on your side. You feel that you can trust him, no matter what happens.

But then the moment fades. Your world pops back into focus. And all your problems, with their messy details and unanswered questions, return with a vengeance. So you sigh, shake your head, and prepare to plunge back into normal life. But in that instant before you fully return, what would you do with the "God moment" you've just had?

Perhaps you might abandon it. You could simply dismiss it as wishful thinking, something no more real than a daydream. Or perhaps you might believe it. You could be firmly convinced that you heard from God. Or maybe you would respond somewhere in between. You might hope that you really heard from God, but you honestly wouldn't be sure.

Regardless of your response, if you want to genuinely have such a moment with God (or want to have these moments more often), then this book is for you. I believe it's possible to have such a moment with God. In fact, I believe you can have a lifetime of these moments, with each one reminding you that God is truly good, that God truly cares about you, and that God will never leave you.

These moments with God have changed my life. And I haven't just experienced them on days when I already felt that life was good. These moments have occurred during stresses at work, tensions at home, strained relationships, and money problems. They've appeared as I've been abruptly thrown into major life changes, like losing a job or having to relocate. They've helped me when I've wrestled with thorny issues, like facing a difficult decision or working through a personal failure.

These moments with God have also shown up on my worst days. Like the day I found out that my father had committed suicide. Or the day I discovered that my wife had terminal cancer. Or the day I was forced to admit that I was burned out and couldn't recover without help. Even on those days, when I felt like my world was shaking, God reminded me that he was still with me and that he was on my side.

If in this moment you can believe God is on your side, then you can face life with confidence and without fear or shame. You can get involved in relationships without being overwhelmed by them. You can take worthy risks and be at peace with the uncertainty they bring. You can have courage to choose the right and avoid the wrong. You can endure trouble or suffering without becoming bitter. If you stumble into wrongdoing (as we all do quite frequently), you can be sure God will forgive you. And when someday you face your own death, you can be at peace because you know you'll spend eternity with God.

But you can't just stumble into that kind of certainty, and you can't force yourself to trust God even if you believe he exists. You must be convinced—for more than just a few moments—that God is for you and that he'll be with you always. Otherwise, you'll always wonder how God feels about you, and you won't be certain that he is on your side.

Unfortunately, we don't find that certainty easily. We all have difficulty seeing that God is on our side. This is not God's fault; it's just the way things are. But God understands our doubts, and he doesn't want us to keep wondering how he feels about us. If you want to be certain that God is on your side, then I believe you are in the right place. Finding that certainty with God is what this book is all about.

CHAPTER ONE

BLINDNESS

A blind man will not thank you for a looking-glass.

—ENGLISH PROVERB

y dad stood at about five-and-a-half feet tall, with blue eyes and wavy dark brown hair that had turned prematurely gray. By the time I finished sixth grade, his hair was totally gray, except for a few hairs at the base of his neck. But he didn't seem old. His face, especially his eyes, seemed younger; it was as if his youthful energy had drained the color from his hair.

Dad valued hard work, respect, and honesty. He was also a hard-driving director. When he commanded, he expected people to respond. If he felt it necessary, he was not afraid to confront someone or chew them out. And although he wasn't physically large, his confidence and tenacity made him seem formidable. His driven nature affected everything he did. He thrived on conflict, and he was fiercely competitive. He wanted to overcome, beat the obstacles, and be the victor.

In contrast, I (Dad's oldest son) was a thinker and a dreamer. I loved to read, and I kept mostly to myself. I was timid in social situations, including sports and other games, and I avoided con-flict. This meant that I sometimes avoided my father.

Still, I greatly respected Dad. And even though we didn't always see eye-to-eye, we didn't have a bad relationship. But we didn't tend to hang out, and it was not our habit to talk for the sake of talking. If Dad told me that he wanted to talk, I would get nervous.

Good Advice, Deaf Ears

During my senior year of high school, I was ready to get out of my parents' house and make my own way in life. I was brashly con-fident that I could make my life so much better than my parents' lives. Never mind that these same parents had given me a home for eighteen years, provided for my every need and many of my wants, or that their finances were sending me to college. I somehow didn't think about that very much. I was just itching to leave home.

Then one night, a few months before my high school gradua-tion, my dad found me and said he wanted to talk.

We went to the downstairs den, a frequent hang-out place in our home. The room had wood paneling, fluorescent lights, and some horrid shag carpet that had shades of yellow and green. But the room was comfortable, the stuffed furniture was well-worn, and there were plenty of amusements: a TV, shelves filled with board games, and a bumper pool table.

But we weren't there to watch TV or play a game. I sat across from Dad and waited for him to start, wondering if he would tell me good news, bad news, or some mixture of the two.

He started with good news. He announced that since I was eighteen and would soon be off to college, he and Mom were going to stop watching over me so much. No more curfews. No more having to ask permission to go or stay somewhere. They would still appreciate knowing my plans, but if I chose not to tell them, they wouldn't get angry. He was confident that I could stay out of trouble. Besides, once I left for college, they wouldn't be so close by, so he said I'd better get used to making my own decisions about what to do and how to spend my time.

As my shock wore off, I thanked him for his decision and for his confidence in me. (I was trying to act serious, but I could hardly contain my excitement.)

I was still in a happy mood when Dad's talk began to take a different track. He told me that I still had a lot to learn. He told me that I probably thought I had life figured out, and that I probably thought I knew more about life than he did.

I didn't dare admit that, but I didn't have to. He probably could read it on my face.

"That's okay," he told me. "I thought the same thing when I was eighteen."

Then he told me to listen and remember some advice. "You'll realize one day that you don't have it all figured out," he said.

Then Dad went on to say many other things. He talked about the hard realities of life. He talked about having to sacrifice to make life work. He talked about how he had to let go of some dreams. And he talked about how in the end, you have to provide for your family, because that's just the way it is.

And here's the sad part. To my young ears, it sounded like he was against me, telling me my plans were unrealistic. At the time, I wanted to be a professional musician, and it seemed like he was telling me to throw my dreams out the window. I tried to listen, tried to understand, but it all sounded so discouraging. I started objecting and Dad got frustrated. Our conversation fizzled and ended without satisfaction.

ON YOUR SIDE TODAY

However, I never forgot that conversation. Deep down, I knew Dad wasn't against me, and I knew he didn't want to squash my dreams. But as I finished high school and went off to college, I remained blind to whatever good purpose he had in mind for that night. Occasionally I would think about his words, struggle with them, and then lay them to rest again, no closer to the answer than when I started.

I never became a professional musician. I loved music but realized I didn't have the talent or the tenacity to make it in the music business. I embraced other vocational pursuits and settled down. Years later, I suddenly understood what Dad was trying to say: sometimes reality just doesn't fit the dream, no matter how hard you try. You still have to make the right choices—the ones that keep your family fed and clothed and provide for those you love. You can ignore reality to chase the dream and everyone will suffer for it, or you can change your dream to fit reality and enjoy a good life.

It was good advice. Unfortunately, Dad passed away before I could genuinely thank him for giving it to me. I wish I had gotten the chance to tell him that I finally did figure it out.

Good God, Blind People

God's communication with us often goes like that conversation between Dad and me. God is the Father, and we are the children; God is really on our side, but we are too blind to see his goodwill. This blindness toward God affects all of us. We struggle to believe God is on our side.

This blindness comes partly from our limited perspective. We typically focus on what's in front of us today and not much more. Although we can plan for the future (and even plan well), it's hard for us to clearly see a bigger picture, much less the whole picture.

You'd think that in our present age, with more information, opinion, and instruction available to us than ever, we would have a better handle on the big picture. But the opposite is true. More than any other period in history, we are painfully aware of how much we don't know about life. We know our knowledge is minuscule compared to the sheer amount of data out there, growing faster than we can keep up. No matter how much we learn, our knowledge, experience, and intuition will barely scratch the sum of all recorded human knowledge, to say nothing of all our unanswered questions about life and the universe outside of human experience.

So we are blind and we know it. We are not even allowed the illusion that we know all of what is going on. We can't see the whole picture. All we see is the little slice that is our life, full of ups and downs, triumphs and heartache, pleasure and pain.

Forced into this narrow perspective, we might find comfort in thinking God has the whole picture in view and under his control. But our limited perspective also makes it hard for us to prove that this same God has our best interests at heart. Does God really care about us? Or does he have an agenda which is sometimes at odds with our true happiness? How can we know?

We could quit trying to find out and live instead for what we can see. We could simply try to make our slice of life the sweetest it can be.

But if we sense that God is on our side, then we'll keep looking for some evidence of God's goodwill toward us. That search will often lead us to a church of some sort. After all, churches are supposed to help people figure out God, right? And church helps some of us see that God is on our side. If we sense genuine love from the church as they teach us about God, then we'll get the impression that God loves us. But if we sense that the church doesn't really like us, we'll get the impression that God doesn't really like us and that we need to change and live right if we want to be accepted.

To be fair, our impressions of church are not always the church's fault. Each one of us is different and responds in vastly different ways. Two of us may participate in the same church, yet one of us may feel God's love and the other may sense God's rejection. Both impressions of God can't be true. Which one is correct?

Maybe what we really need is for God himself to bridge the gap between our limited understanding, our limited knowledge, and our various religious experiences. Maybe God could take some initiative and reveal his heart to us in a way that breaks into our perspective.

But this leads us to the other part of the problem: even when God deliberately reveals that he is on our side, we don't tend to believe him.

Stubbornly Blind

Isaiah was a prophet who lived in Palestine about 750 years before Jesus was born. For generations, the nation of Israel had been split into two kingdoms: the larger northern kingdom, still called Israel, and the smaller southern kingdom called Judah. Isaiah lived in Judah, which included the city of Jerusalem, the home of the temple of God.

God began to appear to Isaiah while the northern kingdom of Israel was being conquered by Assyria. Things looked bleak for Israel, and the people knew that once Assyria was done with Israel, they would turn their attention toward Judah. Would God tell Isaiah that Judah and Jerusalem would remain safe? Would God give Isaiah a message of deliverance for the people?

Unfortunately, no. Isaiah prophesied to the people that Judah, too, would eventually fall. God's words to them reveal how blind our own minds can become toward God.

> "Go! Say to these people: Keep listening, but do not understand; keep looking, but do not perceive. Make the minds of these people dull; deafen their ears and blind their eyes; otherwise they might see with their eyes and hear with their ears, understand with their minds, turn back, and be healed."
>
> —ISAIAH 6:9b-10

At first glance, these words seem to say God didn't want Judah to understand. He wanted them to be blind and deaf to the truth so they would miss the chance to be healed. Therefore, he told Isaiah to tell the people so. "Listen to me, but you won't understand what I'm saying. Look at me, but you won't perceive what I'm trying to show you."

But that's sort of like poking a sleeping person with a stick while telling them not to wake up. If God really wanted to prevent the people from seeing the truth, there were much easier methods he could have used—such as sending Isaiah far away or having Isaiah take a vow of silence. If Isaiah kept talking about it, then some of his hearers might actually figure out that they need to turn back to God, and if they did that, then God would heal them!

That was the point, of course. God's intent was to stir up the people, trying to make them see, make them hear, make them understand. God knew it would be mostly useless. Only a few would truly hear. Most would mentally plug their ears and keep on going their own way. It was what they had always done.

For over five hundred years, God had openly revealed himself to the people of Israel. He delivered them out of their slavery to the nation of Egypt. He gave them a new land to enjoy as their own. And God showed them how much he wanted them to be his people and how much he wanted to be their God. God taught them how they could know him, how they could relate to him, and how they could live in a way that would be pleasing to him and most beneficial for them. In fact, God promised that if the people would follow his instructions and be faithful to him, then he would bless them beyond any other nation on earth. They would have the life they always dreamed of.

> Now if you faithfully obey the LORD your God and are careful to follow all his commands I am giving you today, the LORD your God will put you far above all the nations of the earth. All these blessings will come and overtake you, because you obey the LORD your God: You will be blessed in the city and blessed in the country. Your offspring will be blessed, and your land's produce, and the offspring of your livestock, including the young of your herds and the newborn of your flocks. Your basket and kneading bowl will be blessed. You will be blessed when you come in and blessed when you go out. The LORD will cause the enemies who rise up against you to be defeated before you. They will march out against you from one direction but flee from you in seven directions. The LORD will grant you a blessing on your barns and on everything you do; he will bless you in the land the LORD your God is giving you. The LORD will establish you as his holy people, as he swore to you,

> if you obey the commands of the LORD your God and
> walk in his ways.
>
> —DEUTERONOMY 28:1-9

But instead of being faithful, the people forsook God. They found themselves swayed by the false promises of those who worshiped other gods. So they abandoned God's instructions and worshiped the other gods instead. Some of the worship practices for these gods were appalling—they involved prostitution and child sacrifice, among other things. But even more than that, these "gods" were just idols and had no power at all. So the one true God had to watch as his own people, whom he loved, turned away from him and trusted in the other gods, who were nothing but wood, stone, or metal.

For God, it was like a slap in the face, like a spouse who discovers their beloved has taken another lover. And his people weren't exactly hiding their unfaithfulness. Instead of just carrying on in secret, they worshiped the idols in open view. They still went through the motions of worshiping God, but their hearts weren't in it. The idols were in their hearts' bedroom; God was moved to the porch.

In response, God withheld his blessing and brought hardship to his people. And they would return to God for a time, but when the crisis was past, they would forsake God again and devote themselves to the other gods even more than before. And with each betrayal their hearts became harder, and their actions became more corrupt and wicked. They were ruining themselves, and God knew it.

> "I am the LORD your God, who teaches you for your
> benefit, who leads you in the way you should go. If
> only you had paid attention to my commands. Then

> your peace would have been like a river, and your
> righteousness like the waves of the sea."
>
> —ISAIAH 48:17b-18

God knew the people who heard Isaiah's message would not under-stand. They would be too blind to see that they needed him. They would be too deaf to hear the message that would bring them hope. Therefore, he basically told them: "I would heal you if you turned, but never mind, you won't see it anyway. So go ahead, be deaf! Be blind!"

Current-Day Blindness

We really can't pass judgment on them, though; we tend to do the same thing. We might not have literal gods of wood, stone, or metal, but we do have idols. We become fixated on things that are more immediate and visible—work, relationships, money, pleasures. These are the idols we serve and worship. And we usually fail to see what's so wrong with such worship and how much harm we are doing to ourselves and others when we make these things our gods.

> Now, I say, whatever your heart clings to and confides in, that is really your God.
>
> —MARTIN LUTHER

While we are pursuing our own idols, God proclaims that we are sick, sinful, and need healing. But again, we don't tend to believe him. Maybe we even wonder why God is so demanding. Why does God care what we do? Why doesn't he just leave us alone?

So if we do find God again, that search usually doesn't begin with a desire for God himself, God's will, or God's ways; it begins with an awareness of need. There is some void or pain or guilt or deep desire in our souls. Something isn't right.

We feel it in the restless stirring, the frantic activity, the sleepless nights. We need something. And perhaps we have tried to find this something in our jobs, our relationships, our possessions, or our enjoyments. And while these may temporarily satisfy us, bring us fulfillment, or give us purpose, the mysterious something-is-not-right feeling eventually returns, and the restless stirring begins anew.

The gnawing need may sometimes become acute. Maybe we lose our job. Maybe a close relationship falls apart. Maybe we fall prey to theft or violence. Maybe someone we love dies. Then we grope with unanswered questions, perhaps even speaking these questions into the air. Do we hope God will answer?

Our trust in God is at the root of this search to meet this persistent need. For if we truly trust God, knowing he is on our side, then nothing can really shake us. But when we place our trust elsewhere, sooner or later our confidence will fail.

Tragic Blindness

For fifteen years, my dad sank his life into the manufacturing business he had started. I watched him develop and grow his business, despite many trials. I admired him for his hard work, perseverance, and success.

I'm sure Dad believed he would run his business for the rest of his working life, and perhaps he believed it would even outlast him. But like so many small business owners in the early 1990s, he ran into tough times financially. He finally had to deal with the reality that his factory could not overcome its debts, and he had to shut it down. It was a major blow.

He tried to rebound by diving into various other lines of work with his typical enthusiasm and energy. But a breakthrough wouldn't happen overnight, and he still had the debts of his former business hanging over him. In my infrequent talks with him, I could sense his frustration and despair.

I thought little about it though; he had always worked things out, always overcome. Meanwhile, I was preoccupied with finishing up college and preparing to get married. And when the wedding day finally came, Dad was there and genuinely happy, wishing us well and saying how proud he was.

But about a month after our wedding, I got a call from Dad's pastor, saying he was on his way to see me. When he arrived, we sat down together and he talked with me about what had happened. Dad had loaded his favorite hunting rifle and with one squeeze of the trigger, he left this life and entered the next.

I can't know what thoughts went through his mind in those moments, but I do know one thing: he wasn't seeing things clearly. It's a tragic irony that this same man who urged me to adapt my dreams to reality was unable to do the same when he faced his darkest hour. I wish he could have seen all the reasons he had to live. There's so much that he has missed.

Most of all, I wish Dad had been able to trust God's presence and goodness during that difficult time. Despite all that had happened, despite how he felt, God had not left him, nor had God turned his back. God was still on his side.

Learning to See

Unfortunately, we all tend to be blind toward God's goodness. When things are going well, we'll often credit our own talent, merit,

12

or hard work more than we credit God. And when things are going poorly, we'll often equate our bad fortune with God's disapproval. No one taught us to assume this; we do it automatically, asking ourselves what we did to make God angry.

What if God isn't that way at all? What if God's goodness toward us is greater than any of our current troubles and purer than any human motives we've experienced? Could we let God rid us of our blindness and open our eyes to see how much he desires to bless us?

CHAPTER TWO

MOTIVES

There seems to be a kind of order in the universe, in the movement of the stars and the turning of the earth and the changing of the seasons, and even in the cycle of human life. But human life itself is almost pure chaos. Everyone takes his stance, asserts his own rights and feelings, mistaking the motives of others, and his own.

—KATHERINE ANNE PORTER

One night I could not fall asleep. I tossed and turned and was generally quite miserable. I finally got up, went into the living room, and flipped on the TV, hoping I could put my restless mind at ease. As I surfed the channels, I was mostly greeted by news, reruns, and infomercials.

I briefly stopped to watch a program that promised its viewers great wealth and the fulfillment of all their desires. This program wasn't offering a new product, business opportunity, or investment strategy. Instead, it claimed riches were available through God's promises in the Bible.

The program urged people to send for a free book and urged them to follow up with generous donations to its "ministry." It assured viewers that if they had faith and gave their money, then God would bless them with incredible prosperity. The appeal was so blatant, so deceptive in its treatment of Scripture, that I just shook my head in disgust.

Even now, when I think of that late-night moment, I am dismayed at how drastically people can twist the pure goodness of God into something so selfish and ugly.

Obscuring the Truth

That late-night infomercial is an example of prosperity preaching, which basically says God will give his true followers health, wealth, success, and security in this world. So if we are not healthy, wealthy, successful, and secure, then we've just failed to follow God. This message shows up all over the place in all kinds of different religious forms. But it's obscene. It's a lie. It's a thinly veiled cover for greed.

But that lie only survives because it's joined to a great and powerful truth. Like a bulging parasite, the lie feeds off this truth and at the same time obscures it. And when the lie is proven false—as it always is—people often throw out the great and powerful truth along with it.

The great and powerful truth is this: God wants to bless us.

That part is true. God wants to bless us beyond what we could dream or imagine. He enjoys blessing us. He is even willing to take extraordinary measures to bring us the best future possible.

Unfortunately, the prosperity preachers try to connect this great truth to material wealth and basic human desires. The resulting message is destructive to our souls. It's idolatry all over again: the prosperity preachers place the glory on the gifts of God instead of God himself.

> As for the rich in this present age, charge them not to
> be haughty, nor to set their hopes on the uncertainty
> of riches, but on God, who richly provides us with
> everything to enjoy.
>
> —*1 TIMOTHY 6:17 ESV*

God does desire to bless us, but the blessing God wants to give us is far greater than money. And every so often, even during our struggles and pain, we catch glimpses of joy that point us back to the God who is at the root of all true happiness.

An Ordinary Flight of Steps

I might never have married Ann if her college roommate hadn't turned me down for a date.

Ann's roommate was Stephanie, a girl with curly brown hair and a wide smile. In the fall of my sophomore year, I'd received some free passes to a movie on campus, and I finally worked up the nerve to ask Stephanie to go with me. I guess she wanted to let me down easy, because instead of just saying, "No, thanks," she suggested I take her roommate, Ann, to the movie instead. I had never met Ann, but Stephanie insisted. "She really likes movies," Stephanie said.

Meanwhile, I was thinking the movie wasn't the point in the first place; it was just a pretense for spending time with Stephanie. Oh, well, sure, I'll go to the movie with Ann. Why not? I like movies too.

So we set it up. I was to come down to Stephanie's room and meet Ann before taking her to the movie. At the appointed time, I walked to where she said their hall was and looked around for a minute. It was a short hallway, with only about half-a-dozen doors. I wanted to make sure I was in the right place.

The hall was deserted except for a girl who was sitting on the floor reading. The girl had long brown hair and she was wearing jeans and a red sweater. She looked up at me and watched me hesitate.

"Are you looking for Stephanie?" she asked.

"Um, yeah," I said.

"I'll get her for you," she said. She got up and ducked into a nearby doorway. A few moments later, she reappeared with Stephanie. "Here's Stephanie," she said. She flashed a pretty smile and held out her hand. "And I'm Ann."

So she had been checking me out. We laughed about that and headed to the movie. (I am glad she didn't decide to make a run for the door.)

That's how Ann and I started out. We went to the movie, enjoyed it, found out we were in a class together, and started studying together for that class. Soon we were going out regularly and spending lots of time hanging out when we probably should have been studying.

I began to feel like I really loved Ann. One day, I got up the courage to tell her so. "I love you," I said.

"Oh!" she said. "That's sweet."

She was not ready to say she loved me. Fortunately, I hadn't scared her off. I tried my best to act like it was no big deal. But on the inside, I was crushed. I wondered if she would eventually feel the same as I did.

One night that November, we were walking back to her hall from the student center. We crossed the street and headed toward Ann's room, which was tucked into a small hallway near the entrance to the football stadium. We couldn't enter there because that hall's outside door was already locked for the night. So we climbed some concrete steps to the left, which wound their way up the hill to the dorm's main entrance. As we went up the steps, talking about who knows what, she suddenly said, "Jeff."

Something in her voice made me turn and look at her. She looked me in the eye, smiled, and with a firm voice she said, "I love you."

That was over thirty years ago, and when I think of it, I can still hear her voice, feel the coolness of the night, and see her smiling up at me there. And those concrete steps, otherwise so plain, became to me a special place.

The spot is completely different now. The university expanded the entrance to the football stadium and completely changed the landscaping. The old steps were demolished. But whenever I look at or think of that hill, I always remember it as it was.

We've all had those moments in life that overwhelm us and make us catch our breath with joy. The world slows down. No anxiety. No guilt. And not a hint of selfishness or greed. For a short while at least, all is right in our world. When it's over, there are no lingering regrets. Nothing to taint the memory.

Pure Delight

I've flown on airplanes numerous times, but not often enough for flying to become routine. One of my favorite experiences of flying involves taking off in the rain. At first the view outside is miserable and wet, but then the plane rises into the gray clouds and finally breaks through to the sun above. It's marvelous. For a while at least, I am above it all, impervious to the dreary world below.

That's sort of how these joyful moments feel. We break through for a while, and then have to return to the dreary and the mundane.

Where do these fleeting moments come from? Why do they feel so right? And how does God fit into them? Does he want us to have them? As the moment ends and we sink back beneath the clouds, do we think we have managed to steal some happiness or somehow persuaded God to give us a little joy?

I believe it's moments like those when we actually catch glimpses of God's delight in us. We don't work up those moments on our own. If God didn't want us to enjoy things, we wouldn't. God made everything in our existence with full knowledge of how we would experience it. He didn't have to give us any enjoyment at all.

So God not only enabled us to feel that rush of life, he intended for us to feel it. He made us to feel it. He created those moments and gave them to us to enjoy. Like any good father, he enjoys giving us good things.

> Every good gift and every perfect gift is from above, coming down from the Father of lights, with whom there is no variation or shadow due to change.
>
> —JAMES 1:17 ESV

> There is nothing better for a person than to eat, drink, and enjoy his work. I have seen that even this is from God's hand, because who can eat and who can enjoy life apart from him?
>
> —ECCLESIASTES 2:24-25

Cheap Substitutes

However, we realize we don't have these moments very often and certainly not as often as we would like. We don't just want to enjoy

Cato Fashions
Store Number: 279
Hikes Point Plaza
Louisville, KY 40220
Phone #: 5024850442

Date: 12/16/23 12:39 PM Store: 00279
Register: 1   Trans: 7844
Cashier: 102
Trans Type: SALE

SALESPERSON NUMBER 102

45448772 J/M Sweaters	27.99
45424321 Plus Drsy Knit T	27.99
SUBTOTAL	$55.98
55.98 KY TAX 6.000%	3.36
TOTAL	$59.34
MASTERCARD	59.34

************3983   I
EARLS/GEORGE

                          AUTH# 11610Z
        Bank Receipt Section
AID: A0000000041010
TVR: 0000008000
TC: 879FF275964FD26D
Application Label: MASTERCARD
Entry Mode: CHIP
Authorization Mode: Issuer

NUMBER OF ITEMS: 2

        THANK

Reta

CATO   EST. 1946

YOU FOR SHOPPING CATO

copy for statement validation.

10027901784412162300010204
SHOP ONLINE AT CATOFASHIONS.COM

Be sure to follow & tag us
@catofashions for style tips,
new arrivals & to share your
favorite Cato looks. You may
even be featured on our site!

Sign up in store for e-receipts.
Saves paper, easy to find
& clutter-free.

Customer Copy

them; we'd like to control them, to summon them when we want. But once we turn toward the experience—seeking it for its own sake, desperately wanting it again—it eludes us. It becomes something else, a shadow of its former glory, a hollow shell. We either realize we can't bring back the past and relegate it to memory, or we become that pitiful person who tries to recreate those moments long after they are gone.

Even worse, we get impatient for these moments. We become dissatisfied with the level of enjoyment God grants us, and we want more. So rather than waiting for the real thing, we often settle for much less. We discover that in many cases, if we make a little deal with ourselves, we can grasp something that gets us close to that pure feeling of enjoyment. Almost. We think it won't cost much; we just have to give up a little bit of our integrity and endure a small amount of guilt.

We think the exchange will be worth it, but the gamble unfortunately never pays off. When the feeling of euphoria fades, we're left with the lasting consequences of our decision to sell out: guilt, debt, addiction, worry. But the most devastating consequence is that it forces us to numb our conscience, which raises our tolerance for accepting the next deal.

> Food gained by fraud is sweet to a person, but afterward his mouth is full of gravel.
> —PROVERBS 20:17

Doubting God's Motives

These little deals, if we can call them little, follow a pattern that was established by the very first humans God created. He gave them a perfect world—including a beautiful garden to live in and take care of—untainted by anything wrong or impure. There was one prohibition: a fruit that grew on a tree in the middle of the garden. They were not to eat that fruit. Anything else they could eat.

You probably know the story: they ate the forbidden fruit. But it's more important to understand why they ate it. They were introduced to the idea that maybe God's motives were not pure; that he had prohibited the tree's fruit because he had a hidden, selfish agenda. Maybe if they would boldly eat the fruit anyway, they would experience a greater life than what God would give them.

> Now the serpent was more crafty than any other beast of the field that the LORD God had made.
>
> He said to the woman, "Did God actually say, 'You shall not eat of any tree in the garden'?" And the woman said to the serpent, "We may eat of the fruit of the trees in the garden, but God said, 'You shall not eat of the fruit of the tree that is in the midst of the garden, neither shall you touch it, lest you die.'"
>
> But the serpent said to the woman, "You will not surely die. For God knows that when you eat of it your eyes will be opened, and you will be like God, knowing good and evil."
>
> So when the woman saw that the tree was good for food, and that it was a delight to the eyes, and that the tree was to be desired to make one wise, she took of its fruit and ate, and she also gave some to her husband who was with her, and he ate.
>
> —GENESIS 3:1-6 ESV

So before the original human sin could take place, humans had to be convinced that God was not altogether on their side. They were led to believe God must be holding out on them.

And here we are, ages later, wrestling with the same doubts. What if God's keeping us down? What if God doesn't want us to become all we could be? What if he just wants to keep us in our place?

Imperfect Models

If the first humans—living in a perfect world and in perfect relationship with God and each other—could doubt the purity of God's motives, then imagine how difficult it is for us to believe God's instructions come out of pure motives. Our very life experience tells us nobody has pure motives. Every person we encounter has a selfish agenda (whether we see it or not), and when a conflict arises between their own agenda and what's really best for us, they often choose their own agenda.

> *We are all selfish & I no more trust myself than others with a good motive.*
>
> —LORD BYRON

We are not really surprised when this happens. Again, it's so common that we think it's normal. Our entire world system, including politics, economics, and social norms, is structured to manage people's competing agendas. And when these structures break down, we fight.

> What is the source of wars and fights among you? Don't they come from your passions that wage war within you? You desire and do not have. You murder and covet and cannot obtain. You fight and wage war.
>
> —JAMES 4:1-2a

If we are fortunate, we will be able to point to some significant individuals in our lives who demonstrated some purity of motive with us. Perhaps we had a parent, a boss, a teacher, or a good friend who consistently acted in our best interest. They taught us to choose wisely. They encouraged us to grow and improve. They weren't afraid to confront us when we did wrong, but they were quick to praise us when we did something right. They weren't perfect (we saw their selfish agenda on occasion), but they tried hard to not let their own desires get in the way.

More often, though, we find ourselves disappointed by the obvious selfishness of others or outraged when others lie about their agendas. We come to expect that everyone is like this to some extent—even those we trust, those closest to us.

Even more disturbing, we see the same tendencies in ourselves. We try to do right and find ourselves going wrong. And then the cover-up begins, the saving face. No, this is not selfishness, we claim. Really, it's not. We have good reasons, and everyone has needs, and we're just reacting to how we were brought up as children. We become very good at hiding our agendas.

All this hiding leads to spiritual blindness. We struggle to see God's goodness behind his commands and instructions. And so, like the first humans, we hide from God.

We must realize God is not like us or any of our imperfect models. God does not have a hidden, selfish agenda. He does indeed want the best for us, even though everyone else's motives, including our own, are tainted with selfishness.

Even worse, by choosing these selfish ways and choosing to disobey God, we've actually embraced death and put ourselves under God's wrath. This doesn't change God's desire to bless us, but it makes things a lot more complicated.

24

CHAPTER THREE

WRATH

God bears with the wicked, but not forever.

—MIGUEL DE CERVANTES

The biblical descriptions of God's wrath are shocking.
In the biblical account of the great flood, God saw that human thoughts were nothing but evil all the time. God regretted making humans and resolved to rid the world of their violence. And so, except for Noah, his family, and a big boat full of animals, God wiped off the face of the earth every man, woman, child, and animal. He drowned them all.[1]

In the biblical account of the conquest of Canaan, God used the people of Israel to judge the evil people living in Canaan, destroying the nations there. God commanded the Israelites to slay all the Canaanites—every man, woman, and child.[2]

There are also plenty of biblical accounts where God used other nations to judge the Israelites when they turned to evil. The other nations attacked them, stole from them, burned their fields,

1. See Genesis 6–7.
2. See Joshua 10:40; 11:12-15.

and laid siege against their cities, causing suffering, starvation, and death.[3]

But most difficult are the biblical accounts of hell. At the end of the current age, unbelievers are thrown into a lake of fire, where they will be tormented forever along with the devil and his demons. An eternity of pain—with no breaks and no end.[4]

I shudder when I think of these accounts, and my mind throws up all kinds of questions. Really, God? You drown and slay and torment? Why? Is all that absolutely necessary? How can you bear to do such things?

And while I know in my mind that such expressions of God's wrath must be necessary, right, and just, that doesn't mean I understand them. Even though I have been trusting in God for many years, I still don't get God's wrath most of the time. That's because I tend to view wrath itself as mean, reactionary, and wrong; after all, when I get wrathful, I'm usually in the wrong.

Imperfect Models (Again)

When I was a child, I was usually unaware of the struggles of adults. It was only as I grew older that I began to glimpse the pressures and problems of that adult world. As a result, I was sometimes surprised by the moods of my parents or other adults. Even if they were usually gentle, understanding, and supportive, there would be times when they were temperamental and harsh. Unfortunately, I didn't yet have the maturity to identify displays of anger that were more about the adult's mood than about what I had done.

3. Examples abound in Judges, Kings, and 1–2 Chronicles.
4. See Revelation 20:10-15.

> Everyone should be quick to listen, slow to speak, and slow to anger, for human anger does not accomplish God's righteousness.
>
> —JAMES 1:19b-20

As a child, I heard the biblical accounts of God's wrath breaking out against people. And without even thinking, I interpreted those accounts in light of my own experience with adults. I brought that same sense of unpredictability into my picture of God. I figured God seems nice and loving sometimes, but if you happen to cross him on a bad day, you'd better watch out.

When I think of those moments of childhood now, it makes me wonder what my current actions are teaching my kids about God. And the more I wonder, the more I want to go hug them and beg for them to realize God doesn't have all my faults.

This Thing Between Us

Thankfully, God's wrath has nothing to do with him having a "bad day." And while we might lose our temper, hold grudges, or even plot to hurt someone, God does not get angry that way. His wrath comes from a pure heart, and it does not negate his love. It also doesn't keep him from wanting the best for us.

Then why does God get angry? Why does his wrath break out at all?

Before we can answer that, we must realize there is an element at work that interferes with our relationship with God. There's a thing between us and God. We often don't sense the thing because we've been immersed in it our entire lives. Indeed, the thing is part of us; it's tightly intertwined in us. We can hardly identify it, much less imagine life without it.

This thing separates us from God because it is opposed to God. It's the only element of God's creation that works against his will and purposes. God calls this thing "sin." And sin has some pretty nasty synonyms: evil, deceit, perversion, wickedness. According to God, it's all the same. And it's contrary to his nature, which is thoroughly good, right, truthful, pure, and righteous.

And unfortunately, we have embraced this thing. All of us, to some degree, have acted wrongly. Many of us haven't done so in any extraordinary way. We've deceived people on occasion to avoid trouble or make ourselves look better. We've often been selfish, but who hasn't? We've crossed a line or two we thought we'd never cross, and now we struggle to stay on the right side of the line. Big deal. Everybody struggles with such things.

But to God, it's a huge deal. This thing has literally killed our relationship with him. He can't overlook it. He must deal with it, somehow. He doesn't have a choice. God's response to wickedness is unyielding. He can delay his wrath, but not indefinitely.

> "You have left me." This is the LORD's declaration. "You have turned your back, so I have stretched out my hand against you and destroyed you. I am tired of showing compassion."
>
> —JEREMIAH 15:6

If we only casually read God's wrathful words in the Bible, we might conclude that God is ready to fly off the handle at any moment and strike us down at the first opportunity. But in truth, God has spent a long time being patient and holding back his anger, even when he would have been just to let it fly at us. We just don't usually see it that way. Again, we are blind. We fail to see what is so bad about ourselves.

But sometimes we do catch shocking glimpses of the sin in our lives, even in everyday circumstances. We pass along some half-baked gossip, meddle in someone else's business, or flirt with someone who's off limits. And suddenly, we see our selfish soul as in a mirror, bared, and we recoil from its ugliness. We either turn away in haste or frantically try to dress our cruelness in something more attractive.

Other times, perhaps less often, we get a closer look. We catch ourselves one day fantasizing, tossing around plans in our head—then we wake up, back away in horror, aghast at the surge of excitement we had about doing such a wicked thing.

Or worse, we wake up one day and realize that we've actually done the horrible thing—the thing we thought we would never do. We hold our head in our hands and moan, "Dear God, how did I get here? Where did I go wrong?"

If this is our own response toward our sin, imagine the response of a totally righteous God toward our sin. He longs to come near to us and have a relationship with us, but he is repulsed and made wrathful (as he should be) by our sin.

This separation between us and God works both ways. Sin separates us from God, hindering us from sensing him and believing him; our minds are darkened and blinded toward God. But sin also separates him from us. Because of God's holiness, he cannot even come near to us in any sort of personal way unless our sin is dealt with.

A Necessary Separation

Israel emerged as a nation after a long struggle with oppression. For generations, the Hebrew people had been slaves of the Egyptians. They were builders for the Egyptian government, providing massive forced labor for whatever construction projects the Egyptian king wished to advance. But when the Hebrew people cried out to God, he sent them a man named Moses. God gave Moses the power to lead the Hebrews away from Egypt and into freedom. As a result, the nation of Israel was born.

Immediately after they were free from Egypt, God led the people of Israel away to Mount Sinai. There God gave Moses and the people the most famous code of law, the Ten Commandments. God's first commandment to them was, "Do not have other gods besides me" (Exodus 20:3). Then Moses went up on Mount Sinai and met with God for forty days.

While Moses was gone, the people got restless and impatient. They were unsure when Moses would come back and began to wonder if he would ever return. So they disobeyed God in a big way: they disobeyed God's first commandment, making a calf-idol that they began to worship as their god. When God saw this, he told Moses:

> "I have seen this people, and they are indeed a stiff-necked people. Now leave me alone, so that my anger can burn against them and I can destroy them. Then I will make you into a great nation."
>
> —EXODUS 32:9b-10

But Moses instead urged God to have mercy on the people. So God relented, and he did not destroy them as he had threatened to do. Later, after confronting the people, Moses pleaded with God to either forgive their sin or hold Moses personally responsible. But God refused to lay the blame on Moses, saying, "on the day I settle accounts, I will hold them accountable for their sin" (Exodus 32:34b).

And when it was time for the people to break camp, God told them, "I will not go up with you because you are a stiff-necked people; otherwise, I might destroy you on the way" (Exodus 33:3b).

God has a visceral reaction against sin. He is God; he is supposed to be wrathful against sin. His wrath against sin involves his very nature as God. And his wrath is stirred up when we humans rebel against him, so God must take precautions to avoid his wrath breaking out against us. When God pulls back from us because of our sin, he isn't being mean or spiteful; he's actually being kind. He knows that if he did not pull back somehow, then his wrath against our sin would destroy us.

Day of Reckoning

Still, God restraining his wrath and putting distance between us is at best only a short-term remedy. God's wrath is a force that is powerful and cannot simply be contained. His wrath must eventually be expressed. There must be a day of reckoning, a day in which God settles everyone's accounts.

This day of reckoning must happen even for those who feel sorry for their sin. A human judge does not have the choice to release the condemned from his sentence, even in the face of great remorse.

> *Acquittal of the guilty damns the judge.*
> —PUBLILIUS SYRUS

To release the guilty from punishment would go against justice and would encourage others to commit the same kind of evil.

God's wrath works in a similar way; his wrath against sin can be delayed, but ultimately it must be expressed. Something greater than the sin is at work, something that exists at the core of God's nature and the nature of his creation. He cannot uphold justice and not punish sin. He cannot walk away forever. He must eventually show his justice by expressing his wrath for the sin of every human, the total weight of all the wrong committed by the whole of humankind.

This is the burden of God's wrath, his completely right and just anger toward those who do evil.

And yet, God does not want his wrath to fall on human beings. When God does act in wrath, he does not take pleasure in it. God does not like having to express his wrath; he would rather express mercy. And when someone realizes their sin and turns from it, God is very pleased, and his heart is tender toward them.

> "Do I take any pleasure in the death of the wicked?" This is the declaration of the Lord GOD. "Instead, don't I take pleasure when he turns from his ways and lives? . . . For I take no pleasure in anyone's death." This is the declaration of the Lord GOD. "So repent and live!"
>
> —EZEKIEL 18:23,32

However, even when God withholds his wrath in mercy, his wrath does not disappear; there must come a day where his judgment must fall. And if that wrath falls on us, the result is destruction. An eternity of pain—with no breaks and no end.

But God doesn't want that for us. He wants to set us free from the burden of his wrath that must fall. He can do it. But it would involve a great sacrifice only he could make.

CHAPTER FOUR

SACRIFICE

You can give without loving, but you can never love without giving.

— UNKNOWN

It was a Wednesday. I remember the quietness, and the dim light, with sunlight peeking around the thick blinds at the back of the intensive care room. Ann lay on the bed asleep. She was thirty-two years old and had been my wife for over nine years. Monitors beeped softly, keeping track of her vital signs; other medical machinery hummed and whirred. I sat down on a stool with wheels, scooted next to the bed, and looked at her, waiting on her to wake.

The last time I had seen her was in the elevator, right before they wheeled her off for surgery. She had gripped my hand and stared at me bravely. Now I was the one staring at her, trying to be brave.

Ann had grown very sick over the previous few weeks. Her illness had begun with stomach pain, followed by nausea and shortness of breath. We had endured doctor's visits, emergency room visits, medical tests, missed diagnoses, and medicines that didn't seem to help. When her symptoms suddenly got much worse, we rushed to the hospital.

While in the hospital, medical scans had revealed a wide scattering of spots in Ann's lungs. The doctors were hesitant to jump to conclusions.

"I don't think that it's cancer," one had said, suggesting it could be an infection of some sort. He felt that lung cancer would be highly unusual, for Ann was young and she didn't smoke. "But we need to be sure," he had said. He recommended a biopsy so they could look at Ann's lungs and remove a tissue sample for further testing. We agreed.

When the biopsy was completed, the surgeon, a big man with a kind face, came to the waiting room. He broke the news gently: Ann had cancer. He then pulled out photos of Ann's lungs. They were filled with tumors. And the tumors could not be surgically removed from her lungs.

Now I was the bearer of this grim news. I wanted to be honest, but how could I tell her? How could I tell her that she would probably die and that our time together was likely coming to an end?

But I did my best. I looked at Ann's face, watched her wake up, saw her smile at me. Through the haze of fading anesthesia, Ann asked me what was wrong. I broke down and cried.

In that moment, if I had somehow been offered the chance to switch places with Ann, I'd have done it without hesitation. I know this because I loved her. Love must take that choice if it's possible. So if there had been some magic button on the wall of the intensive care unit that would have taken her cancer away from her and given it to me, I would have pushed that button myself. I would have slammed it home and held it down to make sure I took every bit of cancer from her.

Of course, that choice wasn't possible. We don't get to make those sorts of choices. But I still wished for that choice. And if I could have made that choice, then six days later, I would have been the one to die. Ann would be living life and I would be gone. Instead, she is gone and I'm still here.

God's Choice

When we became separated from God due to our sin, God knew our condition was even more hopeless than a terminal disease. To God, we were already dead, separated from him and under his wrath because of our sin. There was nothing we could do to fix the situation. We were lost and without hope, forever alienated from God, unless God made the choice to save us.

And unlike my situation with Ann, this was not a theoretical choice. There was a real option open to God. And he knew if he took that option, then some of us would indeed be saved, and we would reconcile with him and be with him forever.

God loved us. So he took the option. Love must take that choice.

However, God's choice carried with it a tremendous cost, so great that it makes my theoretical button-on-the-wall choice look easy. But the idea behind the choice is the same. Just as I would have chosen to take Ann's cancer and suffer it myself, so God chose to take his own wrath for our sin and suffer it himself.

And to do that, God had to become a human being. Not just the appearance of a human, but a real human—with all the human limitations. At the same time, he would remain fully God, with his total pureness of character and conduct. Only then would he be able to suffer God's wrath for our sin, taking the punishment that we deserved. This is exactly what God did through Jesus Christ.

An Incomprehensible Sacrifice

God's wrath alone is difficult for us to understand. So it's doubly difficult to understand how God was able to suffer that wrath on our behalf, much less imagine how much that choice cost him. We can make more sense of it when we understand God as the Trinity, that is, three persons in one. We can then see how it's possible that God could logically both administer and suffer his own terrible wrath.

But the details of Christ's incarnation and his suffering for sin will forever be beyond our comprehension. None of us has ever had experience being God. We can't possibly know what it was like for God to become human and suffer for our sin. We can only listen to God's revealed testimony about the choice he made.

The prophet Isaiah described this choice of God to the nation of Judah seven hundred years before Jesus:

> But he was pierced for our transgressions; he was crushed for our iniquities; upon him was the chastisement that brought us peace, and with his wounds we are healed. All we like sheep have gone astray; we have turned—every one—to his own way; and the LORD has laid on him the iniquity of us all.
>
> —ISAIAH 53:5-6 ESV

Jesus himself described this choice of God to a man named Nicodemus, who visited him one night:

> For God loved the world in this way: He gave his one and only Son, so that everyone who believes in him will not perish but have eternal life. For God did not send his

> Son into the world to condemn the world, but to save the
> world through him.
>
> —JOHN 3:16-17

The apostle John explained this choice of God in a letter to those in the first-century church:

> God's love was revealed among us in this way: God sent
> his one and only Son into the world so that we might
> live through him. Love consists in this: not that we loved
> God, but that he loved us and sent his Son to be the
> atoning sacrifice for our sins.
>
> —1 JOHN 4:9-10

These are just three examples found in the Bible that explain the choice God made. There are dozens of other Bible passages that describe God's decision to restore sinful people to himself through his Son Jesus. There are hundreds of other Bible passages that demonstrate God's holiness, human sinfulness, and/or God's desire to reconcile with sinful humans.[5] In Jesus's death on the cross, God simultaneously proclaimed the righteousness of his wrath and the truthfulness of his love. Jesus absorbed the wrath, endured that suffering, and bought our freedom.

Again, there's no way we can truly understand what Jesus went through on the cross. How mysterious to us is the sacrifice of Jesus, suffering the agony of God's wrath poured out on him! How did he do it? How much did it hurt? We don't know. We can't measure that level of suffering.

---

5. For examples of these Bible passages, see chart in Appendix B.

But neither can we measure the depth of God's love for us. That love is beyond our comprehension. Despite our sin, God didn't leave us to perish. Instead, God paid the price to heal us. And in doing so, he showed how truly precious and valuable we are to him.

> But God proves his own love for us in that while we were still sinners, Christ died for us.
>
> —ROMANS 5:8

To some, Jesus Christ dying on the cross seems foolish. They dismiss it from their minds and go about their lives. But to others, the apparent foolishness of the cross makes them stare at Jesus even harder. What is God up to? What does this mean? And if they keep staring until they see how Jesus's death on the cross was God's sacrifice on their behalf, then Jesus's death begins to make sense to them, and Jesus's resurrection gives them eternal hope.

A Hope that Cannot Die

Back in that intensive care room, through my tears, I somehow got through telling Ann about the cancer that was eating her lungs, robbing her of oxygen, taking her life. I was as honest as I could be. I held her hand, told her I was sorry, told her I loved her. There was nothing more I could do. No magic button on the wall.

Then Ann said, "Jeff, witness to me."

I knew what she meant: she wanted me to tell her the good news of Jesus. I wondered why. She already knew the good news, and she had believed in Jesus since she was a child. Was she doubting? Was she uncertain about her relationship with God? Or did she just want to hear the good news again?

But I didn't ask questions; I simply told her the good news. We are all sinful; we do wrong in the eyes of God. God has to punish sin. Jesus came and died on the cross, taking our punishment for us. Anyone who believes in Jesus will receive God's forgiveness and eternal life—and when they die, they will go to heaven and be with Jesus forever.

Ann listened intently, as if for the first time. I almost choked up on the death-and-heaven part. But after I finished, I realized I need not have worried about her relationship with God. For Ann simply nodded, looked up into my eyes, and smiled.

CHAPTER FIVE

FAITH

That we ought, once for all, heartily to put our whole trust in God, and make a total surrender of ourselves to Him, secure that He would not deceive us.

—BROTHER LAWRENCE

Because of Jesus's sacrifice on the cross, God's wrath for our sin has been satisfied. But that doesn't mean we are all automatically reconciled to God. Reconciliation can't be forced. For that full reconciliation to happen, we must each respond to God in faith. But this step of faith is shorter than we might think and much shorter than some Christians have made it out to be.

To show what I mean, allow me to tweak an illustration about Christian faith that has been around for a long time. It's called the "bridge." For the most part, the bridge illustration is a good way to demonstrate what it means to trust in Jesus. But the illustration also has a weak spot, and so I'd like to explain it in a slightly different way.

The Bridge

The bridge illustration starts with God on one side and us on the other. A bottomless gulf lies between. Our sin is the reason for this great divide between us and God. That's easy to visualize, easy to grasp (and easy to draw on a napkin).

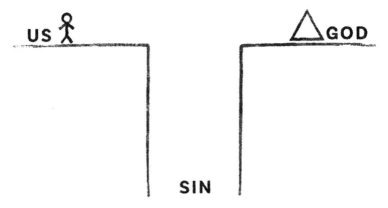

Then a cross is drawn across the great divide, forming a bridge between God and us. This demonstrates what Jesus did for us on the cross. Jesus died to bridge the separation between us and God. His death on the cross and his resurrection from the grave make it possible for us to be reunited with God.

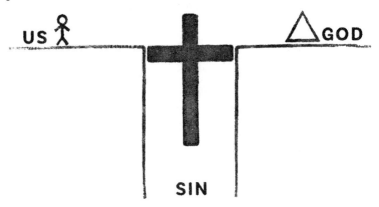

Many versions of this illustration finish up with an arrow drawn from our side to God's side, showing how we can choose to believe in Christ and come back to God.

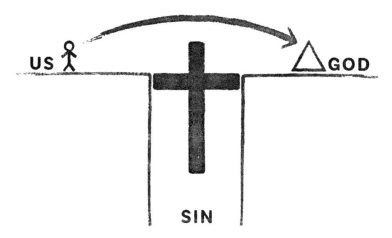

But it's at this final point that the illustration falters—for two reasons.

First, the arrow emphasizes our part too much. We do have a choice when it comes to Jesus, but the arrow makes it seem like we must choose Jesus and then cross the great divide before we are truly reunited with God. And the more we realize how much our sin clearly separates us from God, then the more daunting this journey seems.

Second, the picture leaves God removed from the point of decision. He's on the other side of the great divide, waiting for us to realize what he's done and make the decision to cross back over to him. At the very moment when we most need him to show up, he's far away and somewhat aloof.

Am I nitpicking here? Maybe. I'm sure these two inferences are unintentional. However, a picture is a powerful thing, and I believe that final picture obscures what's really going on in that brilliant moment when we decide to believe in Jesus.

God went on the quest to reach us, not the other way around. We didn't start seeking God on our own. Even with Jesus's sacrifice, we had no hope of finding God by ourselves. Our sinful ways disoriented us, and we wandered blindly, unaware and uncaring how far we were from God. If God had left us alone, we would have lived our entire life without ever finding him.

But Jesus's death made it possible for God to make his way over to us. God no longer has to distance himself from us. Because of the sacrificial bridge created by Jesus, God draws near to us for our salvation. God is the one who has moved to close the gap.

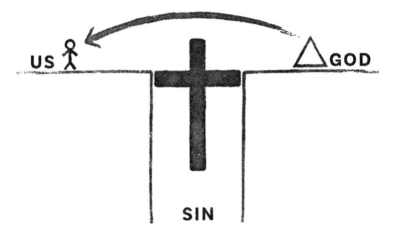

This picture better illustrates God's pattern toward us. God has always been the one to move toward humans and invite them to be with him and trust him for salvation and blessing. We can see this pattern over and over in the Bible, even before Jesus arrives on the scene. Here are just a few examples:

- God went to Noah and invited him to be saved from the coming worldwide flood (Genesis 6).
- God went to Abram (Abraham) and invited him to move to

the land that God would give his descendants (Genesis 12).

- God went to Moses and invited him to save the Israelites from slavery (Exodus 3).
- God went to Joshua and invited him to conquer the land God promised to the Israelites (Joshua 1).
- God went to David and invited him to become king of Israel and establish the royal family that would lead to Jesus (1 Samuel 16:10-13; 2 Samuel 7).
- God went to Isaiah and invited him to proclaim a message that would eventually be recognized as a prophecy about Jesus's sacrifice (Isaiah 53).

God didn't wait for any of these people to come to him. He went to them. And although he may have had different tasks in mind for each of them to accomplish, the core of his invitation was the same: "Come with me, trust in me. I will bless you, and you will see my salvation."

Jesus's coming was the ultimate expression of God's desire to come near to us. In the person of Jesus, God completely entered our human experience. And Jesus didn't establish his ministry and then wait around for people to approach him. He pursued people, breaking into their experience and inviting them to God. But his invitation was a bit different from the prophets before him. The prophets invited people to turn to God to be healed; Jesus invited people to turn to *him* to be healed.

> Come to me, all of you who are weary and burdened, and I will give you rest. Take up my yoke and learn from me, because I am lowly and humble in heart, and you will find rest for your souls.
>
> —MATTHEW 11:28-29

God himself is fully invested in our being reconciled to him. When our sin separated God from us, God made a way to bridge the divide. And God didn't make this bridge and then merely send over an invite! He made the bridge and then he himself crossed over. Jesus does not stand on the other side of a great gulf; he stands right in front of us. He invites us to recognize him as God, take his hand, and be restored to him forever.

And if we really grasp some of the magnitude of what God has done to reach us, then we won't respond with a cold acceptance. Our mind and heart will ignite with love and gratefulness toward God.

Recognizing the Proposal

A few months after Ann passed away, I moved to New Orleans to finish a graduate degree that I had laid aside years earlier. I was a full-time student again. I was also living hundreds of miles from anyone I knew, so I became acquainted with a whole new group of people that had no previous connection with my life. Some of those people became my friends.

Emily was one of those friends. She was a fellow student at my school, and we attended the same church. When I first met Emily, my grief over Ann was still fresh, and I was not interested in dating anyone. But Emily and I quickly developed an easygoing relationship, and we frequently spent time together with the rest of our friends at school or church.

I eventually worked through my grief to the point where I thought I was ready to date again. I became interested in another woman in our church who was attending a different school. I decided to go for it and asked her out. She said yes, and we went out a couple of times, but it felt awkward, and the relationship went nowhere. We mutually agreed to call it quits, and I wondered if it was still too soon for me to be dating anyone.

Then something unexpected happened one night as I was saying goodbye to my friend Emily in the parking lot of our church. She was in the driver's seat of her car, with the window framing her face and her short brown hair; I was standing outside her door. As we said good night, she gave me this look—a smile that was somehow different from every other smile she had given me. It had me wondering all the way home: what just happened?

Whatever it was, suddenly we were spending a lot more time together. For a while, we delayed trying to figure out exactly where our relationship was going. But we finally had to admit that we were more than friends and from that point our relationship deepened quickly.

Having been through courtship before, it wasn't new territory for me; even so, I was surprised at how new it felt. I experienced the same questions, the same nervousness, and the same awkwardness in discussing the future. I kept hoping, yet I tried not to hope too much lest it all come crashing down.

It didn't come crashing down. In fact, a few months later, I realized I had all my questions answered and I was ready. So when I traveled to Georgia to visit family, I went to a jeweler and bought an engagement ring. I started thinking about what to say to Emily to make the moment truly meaningful.

The day I got back from my trip, I went to see Emily in her apartment. She had planned a special dinner to celebrate my return. So I sat down at the table in the dining nook next to the little kitchen and talked and laughed with Emily as she finished up her pot roast. Meanwhile, the ring was burning a hole in my pocket. I hadn't planned to have the ring with me, but I hadn't gone home, and I didn't want to leave it in the car. I thought, why wait? I love her. And I'm sure about this.

So during dinner, I slid into a speech and started telling her all the ways she was special to me. I was leading up to the big moment, but she didn't have a clue what was going on. In fact, at one point a bell rang from the kitchen, signaling the blueberry dessert had finished baking, and she said, "Oh, hold that thought," and went to take care of it. She had no idea at all that I was about to ask her to marry me.

So the actual moment was a total surprise to Emily. She just thought I was saying nice things about her and about us. But when I pulled out the ring box, her gaze locked on the box, and in her mind all my carefully chosen words turned to *blah-blah-blah*. She suddenly realized what I was doing because she knew what that box meant! She couldn't wait for me to open it. When I finally stopped talking, opened the box, and asked the question, she said yes.

Recognizing Jesus's Offer

In the same way, if we really come to believe in Jesus and genuinely recognize his sacrifice on the cross, then at some point we'll respond to him. We'll be thinking of the cross and suddenly everything else will go blurry, because we'll understand what he did and what he's offering. We'll realize what he has done for us, we'll believe he really loves us, and we'll want to leave our old life to be with him. So we'll say yes and give him our hand. We'll accept his gift of eternal life and join ourselves to Jesus forever.

Or not.

We could refuse Jesus's offer. But if we do, we must understand the nature of that refusal. We would not simply be ignoring an invitation sent from afar. We would not just be declining to RSVP for the afterlife. We would be refusing the God who loves us and ignoring the one who suffered greatly to reach us. He stands before us, offering us deliverance from hell and a restored relationship with God, bearing the scars in his body from the sacrifice he made for us. And if we refuse him, then we would be rejecting his love and sacrifice and placing ourselves back under his wrath.

So if we sense that Jesus is drawing close and inviting us to himself, we dare not treat him lightly. We shouldn't simply find reasons to put him off. Faith may not come easily, but if Jesus's claims can possibly be true, then we surely must give him a hearing.

Our consideration of Jesus's offer is the opposite of the temptation in the garden of Eden. Instead of innocent humans considering an offer of evil, we are sinful humans considering an offer of amazing grace. We've all accepted the first offer. What will we do with the second?

We are often skeptical of those who love us the most. From childhood, we tend to distrust those who claim to be instructing us in love, keeping us from danger, and leading us on the path of life. Maybe that's one of the reasons God appointed the good news about Jesus to be spread by flawed, messy, inconsistent human beings. We tend to listen to one another far more than we listen to God.

> *Thus wishing to appear openly to those who seek him with all their heart and hidden from those who shun him with all their heart, he [Jesus] has qualified our knowledge of him by giving signs which can be seen by those who seek him and not by those who do not.*
>
> —BLAISE PASCAL

I am just one of those flawed, messy, inconsistent human beings. So if you hear and understand the message I'm sharing about Jesus, and if you feel drawn in and want to believe, then know that all of that is not really coming from me. It's coming from God.

CHAPTER SIX

HAPPINESS

At the cross, at the cross where I first saw the light,
And the burden of my heart rolled away,
It was there by faith I received my sight,
And now I am happy all the day.

—RALPH HUDSON

hen I was about twenty years old, I wrestled with the question of whether I truly had faith in Christ. As a child, I had simply trusted in Jesus and his sacrifice for me at the cross. But I was no longer a child, and I was finding it difficult to reconcile my childhood decision with my adult life. I claimed to know God, but I knew I still struggled with many sinful thoughts, words, and actions. Did I really believe in Jesus or was I just fooling myself? Reading the Bible, going to church, and praying didn't seem to help. Doubts continued to plague me.

One day, I was driving alone around my college town of Athens, Georgia. I can't remember whether I was headed anywhere in particular. But I do remember having an intense discussion with myself in the car about my faith in Jesus. Back and forth my mind went, trying to figure out if my faith was real.

I finally reached a critical point. I was driving north on a street called Alps Road and edged my car into a left turn lane at a road called Broad Street. It was at that moment that I asked myself a desperate question: was Jesus able to forgive my sin and change my life?

My response (to myself) was, "Of course he is able!"

I remember laughing out loud. And by the time I turned left on Broad Street and headed west, my doubt had vanished. I was reassured and happy, and since then, I haven't seriously wrestled with my faith in Jesus.

What happened? In a word, *surrender.* All it took was one good moment where I focused on Jesus instead of myself.

A Joy Unique

At this point, let me offer a disclaimer: this chapter will make a lot more sense if you found yourself nodding at the end of the last one. If you've already decided to take Jesus at his word and embraced him as the God of your life, then you may find this chapter easier to comprehend because you're already committed to Jesus. But if you're keeping Jesus at arm's length, not willing yet to believe in him and follow him, then you will probably have to work harder to imagine the kind of happiness I describe here.

But either way, if you want to hear more about the unique joy Jesus offers, read on. Because no matter our level of belief, we all struggle to realize God is on our side and that we can find happiness in Jesus. To complicate this, there are plenty of religious people who question whether happiness should even be part of following Jesus.

Happiness vs. Holiness

"God doesn't want you to be happy. He wants you to be holy."

I first heard those words in college. The church I was attending would sometimes host a revival, which meant at least several evening church meetings in a row. These meetings had distinctive preaching and music, which were supposed to be more special than our regular preaching and music. Revivals were common in Georgia at that time, and lots of people enjoyed going to them. (Looking back now, I marvel how we had the time to go to church night after night.)

At any rate, for one of these revivals, my church brought in a team that provided all the music, preaching, and other elements to the revival. And the aforementioned phrase was frequently on the lips of the revival team: "God doesn't want you to be happy. He wants you to be holy." They would say it with such awe, as if they were revealing a secret. Some people would nod and act like they understood, but I would mentally scratch my head and wonder how they could say that about God.

I knew God wanted me to be holy, but I also knew God cared about me. And when you care about someone, you want them to experience happiness. As the revival went on, I began to see that the picture of God they portrayed was very different from the God I knew. I loved God and I loved my church, but I eventually had to reject the overall message of the revival team, which focused more on keeping God's rules than developing a genuine relationship with Jesus.

Over the years, I've heard similar messages about God and happiness. The teaching takes different forms, but it always implies that happiness itself is somewhat frivolous and our personal happiness is really not that important to God, so it would be better if we just discarded the idea of being happy and focused on more important things.

There are probably good intentions behind such teaching. The pursuit of happiness apart from God often lands us into trouble. Sin promises happiness, but its pleasure is temporary and always comes at a price. So we should never assume God wants us to have something just because we think it will make us happy. The thing we are pursuing might actually be keeping us from following God. If so, then we should forsake the temporary happiness of that particular thing and follow God instead.

But that does not mean we should forsake the idea of happiness, even if we have good intentions behind such an approach. Nowhere in the Bible does it assert that God is against our happiness. So we should not pit happiness against holiness as if the two are at war or have nothing in common. We need not have to choose between being miserably holy or happily sinful.

> The happiness for which our souls ache is one undisturbed by success or failure, one which dwells deep within us and gives inward relaxation, peace, and contentment, no matter what the surface problems may be.
> —BILLY GRAHAM

A Deeper Kind of Happy

The problem is not that God is against our happiness—it's that our views on happiness are often too shallow. If we view happiness as perpetual ease, as if the slightest discomfort could come along and ruin it, then we'll never have happiness for very long, no matter how hard we pursue it. Our happiness will be at the mercy of circumstances, fragile and easily lost. That is not the kind of happiness God has in mind for us.

God wants us to have a robust happiness that doesn't vanish in the presence of negative feelings or circumstances. He wants us to be enduringly happy, consistently glad, and persistently joyful. This kind of happiness withstands the circumstances and overcomes them. This kind of happiness looks at the whole picture of one's life and is satisfied.

Some Christians prefer to call this enduring satisfaction *joy* instead of *happiness*. If that works better for you, then call it joy. I treat the words joy and happiness as equals because in the flow of life they are indistinguishable. When someone attempts to describe one of them, they almost always mention the other.

Whether we call it happiness or joy, the key to this deeply satisfying experience is delighting in something—or someone. And our joy doesn't have to vanish when our delight mixes with hardship, sadness, or other difficult feelings. If the source of our delight remains, we can still be happy.

Joy (noun)

1a: *the emotion evoked by well-being, success, or good fortune or by the prospect of possessing what one desires: delight.*
1b: *the expression or exhibition of such emotion: gaiety.*
2: *a state of happiness or felicity: bliss.*
3: *a source or cause of delight.*

Happiness (noun)

1a: *a state of well-being and contentment: joy.*
1b: *a pleasurable or satisfying experience.*
2: *felicity, aptness.*
3: *obsolete: good fortune: prosperity.*

—*MERRIAM-WEBSTER DICTIONARY*

Defining Our Happiness Differently

We can experience this kind of enduring happiness once we truly believe the good news of Jesus. The good news of Jesus helps us realize God loves us, enjoys giving us good things, and wants us to have abundant life. We tend to have some very happy moments when we first come to understand the good news of Jesus and genuinely trust in him.

However, our initial euphoria at being united with God through Jesus Christ will eventually fade. Our enduring happiness must be developed through our ongoing relationship with God, and this relationship often feels strange to us. At times, we may not even feel like we're experiencing much happiness through what God is doing.

But if we keep coming back to Jesus, renewing our trust in him, then a curious thing will happen: we will start defining our happiness differently. These new ways of happiness won't instantly appear, fully formed, but they will grow. And as they grow, our old happiness based on circumstances will wither and fade, and our new happiness based on our relationship with God will put down roots and grow strong.

How do we develop this satisfying relationship with God? Most Christian leaders will answer this question by pointing to several practices, including joining a local church, attending worship services, reading the Bible, praying to God, finding a Bible study group, and telling others about Jesus. All these practices are essential and good.

However, many Christians participate in such practices and yet find themselves constantly hampered by a lack of joy. That's because these practices alone will not produce a satisfying relationship with God; we can participate in these practices to some extent without engaging our hearts toward him. However, if we do engage our hearts toward God, these practices (among others) can help us develop the two habits of trusting God and obeying God. These two habits build and strengthen our enduring happiness with God. We'll never become good at this kind of happiness unless we develop both habits, and we'll always be limited by the weaker of the two.

One Leg Is Not Enough

Some years ago, while on vacation, I went with my kids and some of their cousins to a trampoline park. I decided to have some fun and jump along with them. I had a great time until the final few minutes of the session, when I happened to come down hard on a stiff trampoline. My right leg buckled, and pain shot through my right knee. I rolled off the trampoline, gingerly walked to a bench, and decided I was done. But the knee didn't swell, and the pain wore off. I thought I had avoided disaster.

I didn't know that I had torn some cartilage and a ligament inside my right knee. Over the next few months, I had moments where the knee felt weak and painful. Did I have these symptoms checked out? No, of course not. I waited until my right knee painfully locked up one day.

At that point, it didn't matter that I had a healthy left leg. My right leg was damaged, and the best I could do was hobble around on crutches. Even after a very successful knee surgery, it took months of rehab before I could walk without pain and tightness. While taking showers, I would often notice the firm muscle tone of my left leg compared to the thin scrawny muscles in my right leg. I had to keep gradually walking longer distances until I could jog and then keep jogging until I could run.

In the same way, just like both legs are required for us to genuinely experience walking or running, our obedience to God and our trust in God must work together for us to experience happiness. Obedience without trust leads to legalism, where we dutifully obey God's rules but without joy. Trust without obedience leads to license, where we mentally believe in God's goodness but without victory over sin. God doesn't want us to simply hop along with trust or obedience. God wants us to develop both so we can experience the joy of spiritually walking and running with him.

> *Trust and obey, for there's no other way to be happy in Jesus, but to trust and obey.*
>
> —JOHN H. SAMMIS

Trusting God is usually our first foot forward. Trust is what starts our journey with God. However, when learning how to develop Christian habits of trust and obedience, it often helps us to focus on obedience first. Obeying God is a much more concrete notion than trusting God. Trust in God is something one *has*; obedience to God is something one *does*. If we already trust God to some extent, then we can lean on that trust to strengthen the habit of obeying him.

Developing the Obedience Habit

When we first trust Jesus Christ, accepting him as God, then we will know implicitly that we are supposed to obey him. He is God. We know we are supposed to do what he says. But our obedience to God begins to feel different once we trust Jesus. Before trusting Jesus, we may have tried to obey God out of duty or obligation; but after trusting Jesus, we'll try to obey God because we love him.

Before, we may have gone through the motions of worshiping God to gain some sense of forgiveness, but after trusting Christ, we'll worship God because he has already granted our forgiveness.

This new feeling will also affect our attitudes toward church and the Bible. We'll want to join a group of people who are trying to worship and obey God. We'll want to learn more about the Bible because we want to know more about God and more about what God wants us to do.

And as we move forward in this renewed relationship with a holy God, we'll become more aware of our sin, the sin Jesus died for. We'll find that we can't excuse our sinful behavior as easily as we did before we met Jesus. We'll find that the same Bible that teaches us more about God also teaches us much about our sin. Some of our former habits may become uncomfortable or downright painful because we know God doesn't like them. And deep down, we know they can't be good for us anyway, because if they were good for us, God would not forbid them.

So we begin to obey God more, because we trust him more. This is well and good, but as we trust him more, the more boldly he will lead us. This dynamic can set us up for some unpleasant surprises because God will eventually put his finger on an area of our life that we'd rather he left alone. Maybe that area will involve how we earn or spend our money. Or how we satisfy our physical desires. Or how we behave in our relationships. Or how we do our job, develop our career, or find fulfillment in life. God will bring that area to our attention and let us know he wants us to change and obey him even in *that*.

And once we are faced with the implications of obeying him in *that* (and after catching our breath), then the questioning will begin. Does God really mean that? Do I understand that right?

How would I even begin to do that? How can God even say that?

Such moments can be agony, but they are also holy. As we sort out the implications of God's command and clarify what he means, then eventually we will be left with a choice: either we move toward obedience, or we step away. We may hold ourselves back from him, unwilling to follow him completely and wanting some final say or control. But God will have none of that. God is patient and kind, but he is not one who bargains. We'll either move forward with him in faith or sputter in disbelief and uncertainty.

In those times, if we remember God is on our side, then it will help us take the step of obedience God wants us to take. The command of God is actually a gift from him, spurring us forward to break through a barrier that is holding us back, one that we might never challenge on our own.

Obedience Brings Happiness

When I first learned that my dad had committed suicide, I went through all the emotions you might expect. At first, I was shocked. After the shock wore off, I was mad. He had left my mom alone and he wasn't going to see his children and grandchildren grow up. He was leaving a legacy of sorrow that wouldn't be overcome for years. How could he do such a terrible thing?

But within all these thoughts, I heard another thought. This thought didn't urge me to justify or rationalize or even understand why Dad had taken his own life. It felt compassionate, and yet minced no words: it told me I had to forgive him. I have no doubt the thought came from God. It agreed with the Bible. Jesus forgave me every one of my wrongs, so I shouldn't withhold forgiveness from my dad.

Over the years, I have managed to find all sorts of ways to

personally resist obeying God. I have avoided God, argued with God, and tried to bargain with God. I've delayed my obedience, diluted his instructions, or only half-heartedly obeyed. But in this case, for some reason, I saw no point in arguing. I simply took a deep breath and made the choice to forgive my dad.

If I had resisted God at that point, I would have gotten stuck in anger. Forgiving Dad wasn't just the right thing to do; it was a loving command from God that brought me to a much better place. A happier place. By obeying God, I was able to move beyond anger and feel sorrow over the father I had lost. That's what I needed to feel in order to remember all the good things about Dad, begin healing from the pain, and be helpful to my family as we grieved together.

Once we remember that God truly loves us, it becomes easier to obey his commands. In the same way, when we obey his commands, we show that we genuinely love and trust God.

> If you love me, you will keep my commands.
> —JESUS (JOHN 14:15)

When we obey God out of love, we are still acting in our own interest, but our interest is now based on trust, not on selfishness. It is only when our trust falters that we lapse into self-centered thinking and try to change God's plan to fit what we want. But if we submit to God, trusting that he is on our side, we discover a freedom and happiness that would have been unattainable without him.

That brings us back around to the other side of walking happily with God: the habit of trusting him. But learning to trust God more isn't as straightforward a process as learning to obey him more. We can't directly increase our trust in God, but we will see our trust grow if we increasingly focus on God himself.

Developing the Trust Habit

As we walk forward in obedience to God, we will encounter tough times. Jesus never promised us a trouble-free life. We'll all have times of struggle, frustration, and sorrow. And during those times, we shouldn't just put on a smile, gloss over our troubles, and act like nothing is wrong. There's no command of God that says we should deny our pain.

However, we can intentionally share our pain with the God who has given his life for us. We can also consciously rest in the assurance that God is still close to us and that he still loves us. The apostle Paul wrote:

> Who shall separate us from the love of Christ? Shall tribulation, or distress, or persecution, or famine, or nakedness, or danger, or sword? As it is written, "For your sake we are being killed all the day long; we are regarded as sheep to be slaughtered." No, in all these things we are more than conquerors through him who loved us. For I am sure that neither death nor life, nor angels nor rulers, nor things present nor things to come, nor powers, nor height nor depth, nor anything else in all creation, will be able to separate us from the love of God in Christ Jesus our Lord.
>
> —ROMANS 8:35-39 ESV

Those words don't try to deny or minimize the suffering in life. Nor do they claim that a believer in Christ is exempt from such sufferings. Trouble and distress, famine and nakedness, danger and sword: these are the perils of our current human existence. And on top of those, the believer must sometimes face persecutions.

Jesus was put to death. Most of the apostles were put to death. So if we choose to follow Christ, we would be foolish to think we will somehow escape any hint of persecution for our faith.

But if we have trusted in Christ, then we possess a fountain of life and love that cannot be extinguished, no matter what comes at us. That fountain is God himself. His Spirit lives in us—and not in a theoretical or metaphorical sense. God is a Trinity, three persons in one: Father, Son, and Holy Spirit. The Bible refers to the Holy Spirit as the Spirit of the Father and the Spirit of the Son, as well as the Counselor, the Spirit of truth, the Spirit of the Lord, the Spirit of Jesus, and the Spirit of Christ.[6] Jesus promised his disciples that the Holy Spirit would come to live in them:

> If you love me, you will keep my commands. And I will ask the Father, and he will give you another Counselor to be with you forever. He is the Spirit of truth. The world is unable to receive him because it doesn't see him or know him. But you do know him, because he remains with you and will be in you. I will not leave you as orphans; I am coming to you. In a little while the world will no longer see me, but you will see me. Because I live, you will live too. On that day you will know that I am in my Father, you are in me, and I am in you. The one who has my commands and keeps them is the one who loves me. And the one who loves me will be loved by my Father. I also will love him and will reveal myself to him.

— JESUS (JOHN 14:15-21)

6. Examples of these references to the Holy Spirit include Matthew 10:20; John 15:26; Acts 16:7; Romans 8:9-11; 2 Corinthians 3:17-18; and Galatians 4:6.

The Spirit of Jesus dwells inside those of us who trust in him. So the source of our delight, the provider of our salvation, is never far away. Jesus's presence is our ultimate reason for happiness.

> I would rather walk in the dark with God than go alone in the light; I would rather walk with Him by faith than walk alone by sight.
>
> —MARY GARDINER BRAINARD

Jesus is still with us in the hard places. He is still with us when others treat us wrongly or oppose our obedience to God. He is still with us when we face consequences over some sin of our own. He is still with us when tragedy seems to strike out of nowhere. And our trust in God will grow in these tough times if we acknowledge his presence and turn our hearts toward him along the way.

Trust Brings Happiness

Shortly after Ann died of cancer, I went through a period of intense sorrow. Her funeral was over. About a week later, I went back to work. Life had to go on. But how could I go on without her? She had occupied a special place in my life for almost thirteen years. Now her place was empty, and I couldn't bring her back. On the outside, I calmly kept working and sorted through all the loose ends caused by her death. But on the inside, I was very sad, and my sadness didn't fade for a long time.

However, I look back at that period of my life with something like fondness. Because every day I clung to God, and he felt very close as I voiced my painful feelings and questions to him.

> The LORD is near to the brokenhearted and saves the
> crushed in spirit.
>
> —PSALM 34:18 ESV

One night, I was lying on our bed and pouring out my soul to God, expressing how much I missed Ann and how sad I was. I cried out, venting my anger, my frustration, and my hurt upon him. I told him, "Lord, I don't understand this. I don't like this. I don't like this at all!" But after a few moments of silence, I found myself saying, "I still trust you. Just help me know what to do."

God kept me going during that difficult time as I repeatedly turned toward him for comfort. A lot of my questions to him were never answered, but I knew he was with me, and somehow his presence was enough. When Emily met me, she was surprised to learn I was a recent widower. "You seem like such a joyful person," Emily told me. It was true, but what she saw in me was the strength of God to enjoy life during my grief. I was actually both grieving and joyful. I was sad to have lost Ann, but I was happy to have God.

When Happiness Hides

Even when we have developed solid Christian habits of trust and obedience, happy feelings may not always be easy for us to find.

For example, our sense of joy can definitely be overwhelmed by sorrow or suffering. But in those extreme times, we're often helped by feelings of helplessness. Our helpless feelings tend to trigger responses of surrender to God, which are exactly what we need to begin recovering our joy. That doesn't mean our sorrow or suffering will instantly disappear, but as our focus turns away from ourselves and back toward God, we will probably feel our joy in Jesus begin to return.

More troublesome are the everyday irritations and bad mental habits we fall into without conscious thought. Such moments are more likely to keep our minds away from godly happiness. Instead of a blow that suddenly plunges our soul into deep shadow, we receive a nudge, an unpleasant feeling, that merely lessens our joy in Jesus. These feelings are usually rooted in anger or fear.

The Bible teaches that most instances of human anger or fear are harmful and should be avoided. Such feelings are almost always influenced by incorrect assumptions, sinful desires, or both.[7] Therefore, for a Christian, the best way to handle anger or fear is to turn away from those feelings whenever possible and surrender them to God. Unfortunately, that's often easier said than done. For a variety of reasons, we tend to resist turning away from our anger and fear.

But those feelings, if left unchecked, can distance us from God and darken the joy we have in Jesus. We may even find ourselves stuck in these toxic and deceptive thoughts as we spiral down into an ever-deepening shadow. All the while, we're still laboring under the illusion that we can figure out our own way back to the light.

Emerging from the Shadow

For years, I failed to address some toxic feelings and deceptive thoughts in my own life. Overall, I felt that I was a peaceful person and a joyful Christian. But at times I would become intensely frustrated, especially when people would complain about things. I also constantly worried that I would overlook something or that things wouldn't turn out just right. These frequent nudges of anger and fear drove me to work long days, long weeks, and long months.

7. See Romans 8:15; Colossians 3:8; James 1:19-20; and 1 John 4:18. The Bible also mentions godly forms of anger and fear, but those feel quite different to us.

Along the way, I learned how to work harder, smarter, and faster. I found that I could get a lot of work done and manage a lot of things at once. But no matter how hard I worked or how much I accomplished, it never seemed to be enough to eliminate my frustration or satisfy my worry. When the demands of work increased and complaints arose, I just plunged back into the work with more effort.

Then one year, something in me reached its limit and quietly broke down. I had no great tragedy in my life at the time, yet my inner outlook had grown bleak and despondent. I knew God was still with me and his presence was comforting, but I felt burned out and useless. I kept hoping and praying for the despair to lift and the struggle to end, but it didn't.

As those months wore on, I shared my plummeting feelings with Emily. I wanted to be honest with her about my struggles, and I hoped she would help me figure out what was going on in my mind. But one day, while I was in the middle of one of those depressing rants, she stopped me. "I think you need to talk with someone," she said. "Someone who can help you better than I can."

So I sought some good Christian-based counseling and God taught me many things through that process. He reminded me that I have limits. He taught me that it wasn't wrong for me to need help. He taught me to look deeper into my anger and fear and realize how unreliable and deceptive those feelings can be.

Most importantly, God reminded me that resolving my anger and fear would not come from trying harder, digging deeper, seeking escape, or discovering some extraordinary spiritual secret. The key was surrender. I had to learn to surrender those nudges of anger and fear to God as they arose, and then return to the present moment with him. (That might sound easy, but trust me, it wasn't.)

After my counseling process was over and I was on the mend,

I found that my frustration and worry had greatly decreased. I overworked less and brought home less stress. I became a happier person than before.

Of course, part of me wishes I could have avoided that dark time in my life. But in the end, it was worth it: I had been forfeiting a lot of happiness by stubbornly holding on to my former ways. God firmly but lovingly tore those ways down, and I don't want to build them back.

Practicing Happiness

As I mentioned at the beginning of this chapter, all these thoughts about happiness in Jesus will make a lot more sense if you've already believed in the good news of Jesus. If you have already trusted in Jesus, then let me invite you to simply pull back from life for a moment and be with him. Practice a moment of happiness. Right now.

Take whatever problems you have on your mind, and temporarily set them aside. Recognize that God is the one who has made you, forgiven you of all your sin, saved you for all eternity, and given you this moment. Remember that he is on your side and wants the best for you. Then just breathe. Listen. Look around you. Recognize God is with you and that you are with him. Thank him. Ask him to help you do what he wants you to do. Then just ease back into whatever you were doing before.

There's nothing mystical about doing this. With practice, you can have these moments almost anywhere: when waking, when reading your Bible, when working, while eating, during a church service, or even in the middle of a conversation. You can savor these moments when times are easy and cling to them when times are tough. If you are a follower of Christ, you can always take a moment to affirm your relationship with a good and perfect God and remember the truth of the good news that you already believe.

Bottom line, if we know God really loves us and that he is still with us, then even in our dark days, we have a reason to smile. And if we know Jesus, there is a time coming beyond our darkest day which will completely fulfill our deepest desires for happiness.

CHAPTER SEVEN

FOREVER

If I find in myself a desire which no experience in this world can satisfy, the most probable explanation is that I was made for another world.

—C.S. LEWIS

Once we believe God is on our side, most of our struggles with him go back to our limited perspective as human beings. Even when he removes our blindness, we still can't see the whole picture of our life. Only God sees the whole, and he will constantly urge us to live for what we can't see yet. Our biggest dreams for this world are shallow compared to the dreams God has for us. He wants us to live for the eternal kingdom, not the temporary things of this life.

Our eternal happiness cannot be attained by building our own little kingdom out of money, career advancement, social stability, fame, or personal comfort. All those things are crumbling away and will soon be gone. Instead, God desires for us to have the deep, permanent happiness of being with him forever. This is his definition of eternal life.

ON YOUR SIDE TODAY

> This is eternal life: that they may know you, the only true
> God, and the one you have sent—Jesus Christ.
>
> —JOHN 17:3

As we realize this, we'll begin to live in greater contentment with whatever we currently have. We'll be free to enjoy the good blessings of life, accepting them as gifts of God—but we'll also be happy to sacrifice the pleasures of this world if God asks us to give them up. We'll consider such losses well worth it if we can point others to God in the process.

And when we encounter the muck of the current life—the irritations, the trials, the suffering, and the sorrow—we can still be genuinely happy. God is still on our side, he loves us supremely, and all our troubles are but passing shadows that will soon fade away.

> Blessed be the God and Father of our Lord Jesus Christ.
> Because of his great mercy he has given us new birth
> into a living hope through the resurrection of Jesus
> Christ from the dead and into an inheritance that is
> imperishable, undefiled, and unfading, kept in heaven
> for you.
>
> —1 PETER 1:3-4

At the root of all this happiness is Jesus, who has promised to end this world someday and give us a world that will never end. Jesus told his disciples:

> Don't let your heart be troubled. Believe in God; believe
> also in me. In my Father's house are many rooms. If it
> were not so, would I have told you that I am going to

> prepare a place for you? If I go away and prepare a place
> for you, I will come again and take you to myself, so that
> where I am you may be also.

—JOHN 14:1-3

I think many people, even Christians, have failed to see Jesus's delight in being with us forever. Jesus took joy in being with people and bringing them back to God. And just like other human beings, he loves to laugh, eat, swap stories, and spend time with his friends. He has known pain and sorrow, and he understands our suffering. But he looks forward to a time when all suffering will be gone and he will be abundantly happy with all those who are his.

Jesus once pointed out that even evil parents know how to give their children good things, so it's unfathomable that God would not give his children good things. But just like children, we won't be able to fully understand this truth until God is finally able to show us all those good things.

Waiting on the Good

Our two kids came to live with us when they were very young. Emily and I had considered having biological kids, but as we became more aware of the needs of foster children in our state, we felt that God wanted us to adopt instead. So we signed up for foster parent training, a requirement if we wanted to adopt through the state foster system.

As we learned more about fostering and adoption, we also heard about the risks. One of the greatest emotional risks was not knowing up front if we would be able to adopt a particular child. Even if the state was actively pursuing adoption for a child, there were no guarantees that we would be able to adopt them. We first had to commit to fostering the child in our home for at least six months. After that, if everything worked out in the courts, then we would probably have an opportunity to adopt them.

We accepted the risks and finished the training. About a week later, the state agency contacted us about possibly taking in a boy and girl who were brother and sister. They had been in state foster care almost two years, and the state wanted to pursue adoption.

So we met with their social workers and listened to them as they told us about the kids. We looked at cute pictures and pored over official paperwork. Then they asked us to make a decision. Would we take them?

Emily and I looked at each other. Yes. We'll take them.

We had less than three days to get ready. Suddenly we were buying beds, dressers, diapers, clothes, car seats, and child-proofing our house. We were very excited and nervous when the social worker pulled up outside our door with two little kids in the back, an adorable boy and girl.

And we had a fine day together. We showed them the house and their rooms. We took them to a local park and had fun feeding the ducks. We played with them until dinnertime, then we fed them, gave them a bath, read them a bedtime story, and put them to bed.

I was wondering what was going on in their minds. Did they understand at all what was happening? Did they feel safe? Would they be able to sleep? These and other similar questions ran through my head on that day and many days to come.

Fortunately, the kids turned out to be very sound sleepers; they rarely had trouble sleeping through the night. But it was obvious they understood little about what was going on. How could they? We were their third foster home in less than two years. As far as they knew, we were just another stop along the way to another strange place.

So Emily and I set up a predictable home routine and tried our best to help the kids feel loved and safe. We spent lots of time just playing with them and going places as a family. And as the months passed, they began to ask—with their own limited under-standing—about what would happen next. Would they stay with us? Or would they have to leave?

We longed to tell them that they would stay with us and never have to be moved again. We wanted those kids to stay with us forever. We wanted to give them more happiness than they could ever comprehend. But we couldn't make promises to them yet, and they didn't have the ability to understand why. All we could do was reassure them that we loved them and that somehow everything would be all right. Meanwhile, we continued to monitor their legal case, and we prayed that nothing would get in the way of us being able to adopt them. We'd heard heartbreaking stories of other foster parents who got close to adopting their kids, only to have their hopes delayed, discouraged, or dashed.

But in the case of our kids, things kept moving along, until the day finally came when we took our kids to an office in the regional courthouse to meet a judge. The judge smiled at us, said a few words, and we signed a few papers. It was done. Our kids were officially our kids, and we were officially their parents. We love them even more now and are so proud of them—and we can't imagine our family without them. Among all the desires we have for them, there's one desire that has never changed: we want our kids to be happy.

But sometimes they don't quite understand that. Like any kids, they get upset about their parents' rules and decisions. We're trying to teach them the habits and skills that lead to a healthy, productive, and well-rounded life; but they often resist our instructions, finding them unpleasant and meddlesome. We're trying to help them avoid the unhappy consequences of making bad decisions, but they often focus instead on what they are not allowed to have. They don't yet understand what adults must do to thrive, but adulthood is rapidly coming upon them, whether they like it or not. So we keep trying to get them ready.

It's like Dad and me, except I'm now on the other end of the conversation. I'm an imperfect parent trying to get my kids to trust me even though my words don't always make sense.

Remembering the Cross

We all struggle to trust God, even though he is a perfect parent. Just like children, we doubt his instructions, wrestle with his commands, and ask him questions that are unanswerable. But God understands these struggles. And I'm sure that as God watches us struggle, he's just bursting to show us just how good the other side will be.

In the meantime, God will ask us to trust him and follow him even when we can't understand. And for our unanswerable questions about pain and suffering, he'll keep reminding us of the cross that he suffered for us. The cross of Jesus eclipses any suffering we might have in this life. If we believe Jesus went to the cross for us, then we must admit God is on our side and we can trust him to resolve our suffering in due time.

> If God is for us, who is against us? He did not even spare his own Son but gave him up for us all. How will he not also with him grant us everything?
>
> —ROMANS 8:31b-32

76

This attitude is the essence of being a true Christian. The true Christian does not merely seek to follow the "Christian way" to receive their promised benefits. The Christian sees in Christ crucified the God of the universe rescuing them from death and giving them eternal life. Upon realizing this, they cannot help but respond joyfully, thankfully, and obediently to him. Christians seek Christ, not just his ways; they love Christ, not just his benefits. And they trust Christ, even when they face difficulties, suffering, persecution, or death.

Christians do this very imperfectly, though. Christ is perfect, but their trust in him is not. Perhaps it's more accurate to say Christians keep trusting in Christ again and again. Even the strongest Christians need to be reminded of these things; it is too easy to forget and live as if God's intentions were less than pure and his promises subject to doubt.

I have so far to go. I still have too many moments where I get frustrated or miserable. In those times, I'm failing to look beyond my problems and see the God who gave his life for me. But I'm thankful God regularly wakes me from my stupor and reminds me that he is still on my side. Jesus died for me on the cross. He rose again from the dead. I always have his presence, his forgiveness, and his eternal life. And my struggles, no matter how bad they become, are nothing compared to the life Jesus is bringing soon.

Happily Ever After

We call what happens after death the afterlife. I suppose that makes sense because it does, after all, come "after" this life. But I've come not to like the word, because *afterlife* sounds as if our current life is the main life and that other life will be an afterthought, a benediction, a final act to the play.

But our current life, though important, is actually just the first part. There are many parts to come, so many that the great Director hasn't even given us most of that script. But he has given us a look, enough to stir our longing for those other parts, which eventually makes us long for this part to end. There is a heaven coming, a happily-after-after. It's so real and so huge that we'll never get to the other side of experiencing it.

I'll see Dad there, and Ann, and every other friend or family member I've lost who put their trust in Christ. Dad won't struggle with any despair there. Ann will be free of cancer. And none of us there will ever die. I'll never be separated from them again.

Best of all, Jesus himself will be there with us, and we'll see him with eyes of flesh instead of just eyes of faith. We'll have eternity to spend with him and one another, diving into all God has for us in the new life.

And the stories. Stories upon stories to tell and listen to, stories of the old life, stories about what we're doing in the new. Countless people to get to know but with no pressure of time on us. A new society to build from the ground up, and with Jesus as the King over it all. How could it not be glorious?

This is the happiness waiting for me. This is the happiness God has sacrificed so much for us to enjoy with him. The worst times in this life can't compare with the good God is bringing. Jesus has just given us a taste, and I can't wait to see what awaits us in eternity.

Some would think it foolish to believe there will actually be a happy ending after all the trouble, pain, and suffering of this world. To some, heaven is a foolish hope in a happily-ever-after. But God's Son has made me foolish enough to believe it. I believe in Jesus.

CONCLUSION

Resonance is the property that causes something to respond to a specific frequency of sound. Pluck a loud note on a string, and if nearby strings are tuned to that note, they'll start sounding too.

In this little book, I've been making a specific sound about Jesus. In my own way, I've attempted to convey what God has made the core message of my life, the firm belief of my soul. I am convinced that God loves us more than we can understand or comprehend—and that for those who turn to God and believe in Jesus, all God's ways, God's will, and God's commands work for their ultimate good.

I still struggle to see his goodness sometimes, but that's because of my own blindness. But when I remember the sacrifice of Christ, his promise to be with me, and the eternal future that awaits me, I am renewed, at peace, and happy to be on this journey with Jesus.

Maybe those thoughts resonate with you.

If so, then I encourage you to open up to Jesus. Admit to him your failings, thank him for his sacrifice on the cross, and ask him to help you follow him. He won't turn you away.

I also suggest you pick up a Bible and read it with the mindset that God is truly on your side. If you've read the Bible before and found it to be confusing and harsh, I encourage you to try again. If you are unsure where to begin reading the Bible, try reading Genesis and then Luke. Those two Bible books contain many foundational stories about God, human beings, and the life of Jesus Christ. (If you'd rather take a more systematic approach through significant passages of the Bible, take a look at the ones I suggest in Appendix B.)

Finally, if you haven't already, I suggest you find some other people who follow Jesus in a real and genuine way. You might find them meeting on Sundays in a church building, during the week in someone's living room, or anywhere in between. Look for a group of people who are in awe of Jesus, who rejoice in God's goodness, who enjoy reading and studying the Bible, and who love to show people grace. Spend time with them, learn from them, and join them in helping others know Jesus too.

THE STRANGER, THE BRIDGE, AND THE EVERYDAY MAN[8]

There once lived an everyday man in the everyday land where everyone else lived. It was the only land he or anyone else had ever known. Inside the boundaries of the everyday land there was so much to live for—or so most everyone said.

Around the edge of the everyday land fell steep cliffs. From below these cliffs rose a thick mist. There was no safe way to climb down the cliffs, no way to see the bottom, and no way to see if any lands were beyond the mist. There were rumors of two other lands: one which was blissful and the other wretched. But the everyday man had long ago stopped thinking about such rumors.

What the man knew was that at some point in his life, just like everyone else, he would slowly or suddenly be drawn to the cliffs and vanish into the mist. People had many names for this common yet disturbing occurrence. But the simplest name for it, and the most honest one, was Death.

---

8. I published the first edition of this short story at *On Your Side Today* (blog), May 5, 2018, https://onyoursidetoday.com/2018/05/05/short-story.

As a rule, the man stayed near the central part of the land. That's where most people spent most of their effort trying to better their lives. The man found that he could improve his status quite well; he had a knack for recognizing and seizing opportunity when it came his way. But even though he had made his life quite comfortable, he could not seem to remove the perpetual unrest in his soul. Real peace and lasting happiness eluded him.

But that was before he met the extraordinary stranger.

He met the stranger through an odd set of circumstances. The man had noticed that the stranger always seemed to hang around one of his friends. One day, the man was in the company of this particular friend (whom the man found to be happier than most). The man then decided to take a walk, intending to be alone with his thoughts. The stranger fell into step beside him.

"Mind my company?" asked the stranger.

"Not at all," said the man, wanting to be polite.

So they set out, and the man found he had ample time to think, for the stranger said nothing for a long time. As they continued in silence, the man began to unwittingly follow the footsteps of the stranger. Suddenly, the man looked up and realized they had left familiar territory and were actually nearing the cliffs and the dreaded mist.

The man was both alarmed and annoyed. Everyone knew it was not polite to wander this way. He was about to open his mouth to suggest to the stranger that they turn back. But just then the stranger pointed out to where the edge of the cliffs and the beginning of the mist could clearly be seen.

"Do you see it?" he asked.

The man looked out. Suddenly the mist where he was gazing seemed to thin a little, and he did see something. Despite his loathing of the mist, the man took a few steps closer. He could plainly see it: a huge column rising up out of the mist, far past the edge of the cliff. The column was in the shape of a cross. Leading up to it, from the cliff's edge to the foot of the cross, was a long narrow bridge.

"I know what this is," said the man. "I've heard people talk about it. In fact—" He turned to the stranger. "Our friend talks about this. He was talking about this when we left. This is Christianity."

"So you know about the cross."

"I've heard the story. God's Son Jesus came to earth, died on the cross for our sins, and rose from the dead. It's fine for some people. But it doesn't help me."

"Why not?" asked the stranger.

"It doesn't make sense to me. I don't see how this cross helps me find peace with God or happiness in life. Besides, why is it standing way out here? If you hadn't led me here, I never would have found it."

The stranger smiled. "That's true."

The man appeared not to hear this note of agreement. "It seems to me," the man continued, "If God is so great and really cares about all of us, then he wouldn't shroud himself in this mist and only provide us this narrow bridge to reach him."

"Well," said the stranger. "You've got it a bit backward. And it's a more complicated situation than you know."

The man wasn't quite sure what to say to that. He looked at the stranger's face and saw no intrigue or deception, only sincerity. He looked back at the cross and the mist wafting over the bridge.

"Once there were no cliffs and no mist, either," the stranger explained. "The land of God and humans were joined. It was because of human rebellion that God separated them from himself

83

and shielded them from his holiness." The stranger pointed toward the cliffs. "A good thing too. If he had not, then all humans would have been destroyed."

"Destroyed. By what?"

"Not by what. By whom. By a perfect holy God, who must judge the wrongs of all human beings. The cliffs and the mist provide protection, but only for a while."

The man's jaw tightened. "And after that?"

"Death. And hell. But God doesn't want that for you."

"And to avoid that, I suppose, I need to start living for God. I'm supposed to leave all I've known and go walk over that bridge."

"Not exactly."

"No?" The man looked back at the stranger. "But that's what our friend does. He goes to church, reads his Bible, and actually tries to live by what it says."

"I'm glad you noticed." The stranger smiled with satisfaction. "He wasn't always that way."

"Did you have something to do with that?"

"Yes. I brought him out here and showed him the cross. I showed him that the Son of God suffered the wrath of God for all his sin, which bridged the gap between him and God. When he finally understood, he took my hand, and I've been with him ever since. Now he wants to obey God, and I give him the power to do so."

The man didn't need to ask. He knew who the stranger was. He looked back at the bridge. "Are you asking me to walk over that bridge and give my life away?"

"Well, let me ask you a question. Why do you think I built the bridge?"

"I suppose it was so we could find our way back to God if we wanted to."

"No one wants to find God on their own. Anyway, I didn't build the bridge so you could come find me. I built the bridge so I could come find you."

The man turned back to the stranger, and he saw that Jesus had stepped toward him and extended his hand. The man looked back at the cross, and suddenly he understood. He looked back at Jesus and took his hand.

* * *

It had been many years since the man met Jesus. He felt that his real life had started that day. Over the years, he tried to tell others about what Jesus had done for him. He knew a few of them had met Jesus and followed him. He wondered if any others had done the same.

Now the man had reached the end of his life, and he was once again by the cliffs, this time at the edge. He was staring into the mist which was swirling thick in front of his face. To everyone back in the everyday land, he would vanish just like all the others.

But the man looked beside him and saw Jesus, and he was not afraid. He looked ahead, and he saw the bridge extending into the mist. He couldn't see the cross. But he knew it was there. And he knew it would bear him safely to the other side, where there was light and joy and life with God forever. Jesus stepped forward, and the man walked beside him, and they disappeared as one into the mist.

WHAT I DID AND DID NOT SAY

When you say something, make sure you have said it.
The chances of your having said it are only fair.

— E.B. WHITE

For the sake of clarity, here are my main beliefs about the God I've been talking about in this book. If you've read everything prior, then hopefully these beliefs have already been obvious. On the other hand, if you've skipped here, then maybe these few paragraphs will help you know where I'm coming from before you plunge into the rest of the book.

I believe God exists. I have never seen God with my eyes or heard his voice with my ears. But I believe there is a God. To be a little more specific, I believe there is one God who made all things, and this God is eternal, all-powerful, all-knowing, all-seeing, and morally pure and blameless.

I believe the Bible accurately describes this God. I believe God had an active part in creating and assembling the collection of ancient texts that we call the Bible. I believe the Bible is true to the nature of God and that it gives reliable descriptions of what

God has done and what he is like. The sixty-six books of the Bible, written over thousands of years, give a remarkably consistent picture of God. I believe God gave us the Bible to reveal things about him that we would not have known or figured out otherwise.

I believe Jesus Christ is God. Jesus declared that he is the unique Son of God who was sent by God and is one with God.[9] The Bible consistently describes Jesus as fully God and yet completely human. I do not claim to understand how Jesus became God incarnate nor how his divine nature works in total harmony with his human attributes. Nevertheless, I believe Jesus is the God he claims to be—the God of the Bible, the same God who created all things.

I do not believe there is a formula for getting God on our side. I believe God is already on our side. We don't have to embrace some mysterious method or principles to unlock God's desire for our good. He already wants us to have the best life possible, and he desires us to experience that life in all its fullness.

I do not believe God always wants to bless us in the way we want to be blessed. This especially goes for things like riches, health, and popularity. God does not automatically support our opinion or approve of everything we want. But whether we realize it or not, God desires for us the greatest overall blessing that we could receive.

I do not believe God's goodness means everything in life is good. There are many things in life that God himself calls harmful and wrong, and yet they continue to be part of our present world. Some of our misery is brought about by the wrong actions of others. Many times, we bring such misery on ourselves. And other times our pain seems to have no defined cause—it just happens. And no

---

9. See John 10:25-39.

matter the source of our pain and suffering, we should not gloss over the suffering or ignore the pain. God wants to be with us through our pain, and he wants to use our suffering for our good—but never does he call the suffering good.

I do not believe God's goodness means we will all eventually end up with God forever. This is a tricky distinction. God is on our side, but he will not force that truth on us or force his blessings into our lives. If we persist in turning away from him, refusing to accept him for who he is and ignoring his generous attitude toward us, then at some point he will turn away and let us continue in our blindness. But if we respond to God's goodness, believing in the good news of Jesus Christ, then he will reconcile us to himself forever, and nothing will ever separate us from God again.

THE TRULY GOOD BOOK

*In regard to this Great Book, I have but to say,
it is the best gift God has given to man. All
the good the Saviour gave to the world was
communicated through this book.*

—ABRAHAM LINCOLN

T he Bible is a blessed book, but it is also a large and complicated one. It is actually a collection of sixty-six books written over a 1700-year period. The first thirty-nine books are called the Old Testament and were written before Jesus was born. The remaining twenty-seven books are called the New Testament and were written in the first century after Jesus was born.

We tend to bring our own agendas to the Scriptures. We look for answers to our own questions instead of simply letting God speak to us. But there's one big question that is very important to God and to us: *is God good?* And when we ask this question, it's almost always meant to be personal: *does God want to be good to me?*

God answers this question in the Bible with more than a simple yes. That simple answer doesn't give us enough to believe in God's goodness in our messy, confusing, and often hurtful world.

Instead, the Bible illustrates repeatedly (in various ways) that these four things are true:

1. God is perfectly righteous, wise, and good.
2. We are separated from God's goodness by our sin.
3. God wants to bless us and reconcile with us.
4. We reconcile with God when we trust his good news of salvation, which is ultimately provided by Jesus's death and resurrection.

The following chart lists one hundred key passages in the Bible. These passages give just a taste of how these four themes appear throughout Scripture. This list also works well as a personal reading plan for those wanting to learn more about the Bible in general.

Description	Bible Section	God is perfectly righteous, wise, and good	We are separated from God's goodness by our sin	God wants to bless us and reconcile with us	We reconcile with God when we trust his good news
God creates a perfectly good world, and he creates man and woman in his image.	Genesis 1-2	1:31		2:16-22	
The first man and woman fail to trust God, and they fall to temptation and sin.	Genesis 3		3:6-11 3:22-24	3:15 3:21	
The first brothers are involved in the first murder.	Genesis 4		4:11-12	4:6-7 4:15	
God calls to Noah, and Noah trusts God. He builds an ark to save his family from a worldwide flood.	Genesis 6-9		6:5-7	6:18-21 9:8-17	6:22 7:5
Job trusts God, even though he suffers intensely. Job's friends are little comfort, but God reveals himself to Job at the end.	Job 1-14, 27-31, 38-42	1:20-22 2:9-10 40:6-8		1:9-12 2:3-6 42:10-17	42:1-6
God calls to Abraham, and Abraham trusts God. He leaves his land of origin for a land that God promised him.	Genesis 12-23	18:23-32		12:2-3 13:14-17	15:1-6
God calls to Isaac, and Isaac trusts God. He continues to believe in God's promises made to Abraham.	Genesis 24-26			26:1-5 26:23-24	
God calls to Jacob, and Jacob trusts God. God blesses him and gives him the name Israel.	Genesis 25-35			28:12-16 35:9-12	

ON YOUR SIDE TODAY

Description	Bible Section	God is perfectly righteous, wise, and good	We are separated from God's goodness by our sin	God wants to bless us and reconcile with us	We reconcile with God when we trust his good news
God calls to Joseph, and Joseph trusts God. Joseph becomes a prominent ruler in Egypt who saves many people from a widespread famine.	Genesis 37-41			39:2-5 39:21-23	
The family of Israel (Jacob), relocates to Egypt during the rule of Joseph.	Genesis 42-50			45:4-8 50:19-20	48:21 50:24-25
God calls to Moses, and Moses trusts God. He tells the Israelites that God will deliver them from slavery in Egypt.	Exodus 1-4			2:23-25 3:7-10	
God powerfully delivers Israel from slavery in Egypt, and establishes the Passover sacrifice.	Exodus 5-15			6:6-8	12:21-28
God makes a covenant with Israel, but the people quickly fall into idolatry.	Exodus 19-20, 32-33		19:20-25 32:7-10 33:1-5 33:18-23	20:2 32:11-14	
God invites Israel to enter the promised land, but the people do not trust God.	Numbers 13-14	14:17-20	14:11-12 14:20-23	14:5-9	14:6-9 14:24 14:30
God judges Israel's disobedience with poisonous snakes, but provides a way for those bitten to be saved from death.	Numbers 21		21:5-7	21:8	21:9

Description	Bible Section	God is perfectly righteous, wise, and good	We are separated from God's goodness by our sin	God wants to bless us and reconcile with us	We reconcile with God when we trust his good news
God renews his covenant with a new generation of Israelites, and Moses dies.	Deuteronomy 4-11, 28-34	7:9-10 10:17-18 32:3-4	9:4-6 9:24	4:35-39 5:28-29 10:12-15 28:1-13	
This Mosaic psalm describes a prayer of trust to the eternal God.	Psalm 90	90:1-6	90:7-11	90:12-17	
God calls to Joshua, and Joshua trusts God along with a Jericho woman named Rahab.	Joshua 1-6			1:3-9	2:8-13
Achan secretly rebels against God, but he is found out and destroyed.	Joshua 7		7:1 7:11-12 7:15	7:13-14	
Joshua dies, and Israel begins the cycle of Judges: idolatry, oppression, regret, and deliverance.	Judges 1-2	2:1	2:2-4 2:11-17	2:18	
God calls to Gideon, and Gideon trusts God and delivers Israel. However, Gideon is ensnared by idolatry at the end.	Judges 6-8	6:7-10	6:1-2	6:14-16	7:7-15
God calls to Samson, and Samson trusts God and delivers Israel. Samson falters and is defeated, but he turns back to God at the end.	Judges 13-16		13:1 16:16-20	13:3-5 15:18-19	16:28-30

Description	Bible Section	God is perfectly righteous, wise, and good	We are separated from God's goodness by our sin	God wants to bless us and reconcile with us	We reconcile with God when we trust his good news
Ruth, a Moabite woman, remains loyal to her mother-in-law through much hardship, and ultimately finds redemption for them both.	Ruth		1:20-21	2:8-12 4:14-17	1:15-17
God calls to Samuel, and Samuel trusts God. He becomes a priest, prophet, and judge.	1 Samuel 1-7	2:1-3	2:27-34 7:3-6	3:19-21 7:7-13	
God calls Saul as Israel's first king. Even though Saul wins some victories, Saul does not trust God.	1 Samuel 8-15	12:7-15	8:6-8 15:22-23	9:15-16 10:6-9 12:20-24	
God calls David as Israel's second king. David trusts God as a man after God's own heart.	1 Samuel 16-31	24:9-15		17:45-47 26:23-24	
David becomes king over all Israel, and God promises him that his throne would endure forever. Even so, David commits some tragic sins.	2 Samuel 1-12		12:1-10	7:8-16 12:13	
These two Davidic psalms describe trusting in God even through terrible circumstances.	Psalms 22-23	22:3-5 22:27-31		22:19-24 23:1-6	22:25-26
This Davidic psalm encourages people to trust in the Lord and not be swayed by the prosperity of the wicked.	Psalm 37	37:7-22 37:34-38		37:23-33 37:39-40	37:1-6

Description	Bible Section	God is perfectly righteous, wise, and good	We are separated from God's goodness by our sin	God wants to bless us and reconcile with us	We reconcile with God when we trust his good news
God calls Solomon as Israel's third king. Solomon trusts God, but not like his father David. Solomon builds a temple to God.	1 Kings 1-11	4:29-31 8:22-27	8:30-36 11:4-13	3:5-14	8:46-50
Solomon introduces a collection of sayings to instruct others in the wisdom of God.	Proverbs 1-9	1:7 9:10	1:29-32 6:16-19	2:6-8 3:11-20 8:32-36 9:10-12	3:5-6
Solomon searches for meaning in life, and concludes that it must ultimately be found in God.	Ecclesiastes	3:14	11:9 12:13-14	2:24-26 3:10-13 5:18-20	
After the death of Solomon, the nation of Israel splits into two nations: Israel and Judah.	1 Kings 12-16		14:7-11 14:22-24 16:1-7 16:29-33		
God calls Elijah to prophesy and proclaim God's judgment on Israel and its kings.	1 Kings 17-22		18:17-18 21:20-22	18:36-39 17:17-24 19:3-18	
God calls Elisha to prophesy and proclaim God's judgment on Israel and its kings.	2 Kings 1-13			4:1-7 4:11-37 4:42-44 5:9-14	5:15-17
God calls Isaiah to prophesy and proclaim God's judgment on Israel and Judah.	Isaiah 1-12	5:3-7 6:1-3 8:13-14	6:9-10	1:18-20 6:5-7 9:1-7 11:1-9	12:1-6
God calls Hosea to love an unfaithful woman and proclaim God's love toward unfaithful Israel.	Hosea	13:4-9 14:9	2:2-13 5:3-6 7:13-15	2:14-20 11:1-11 13:14 14:4-7	6:1-3 14:1-2

Description	Bible Section	God is perfectly righteous, wise, and good	We are separated from God's goodness by our sin	God wants to bless us and reconcile with us	We reconcile with God when we trust his good news
God calls Jonah to proclaim God's judgment on Nineveh, an Assyrian city. Jonah tries to avoid the assignment and flees from God.	Jonah	4:10-11	1:2	4:2	3:5-10
God calls Micah to proclaim God's judgment on Israel and Judah, and to prophesy that one day God would restore his people.	Micah	6:1-8	3:1-4 7:2-4	2:12-13 4:1-7 5:2-4 7:18-20	7:7
Israel is conquered by Assyria, just as God's prophets had foretold.	2 Kings 14-17		17:7-12 17:14-20	17:13	
God calls Isaiah to prophesy about a special servant-king who would save God's people from their sins and establish an eternal kingdom.	Isaiah 40-61	40:3-8 40:27-28 45:18-25 46:8-13	59:1-2	48:17-19 52:7-10 53:1-12 61:1-9	40:29-31 55:6-7
God calls Jeremiah to proclaim God's judgment on Judah.	Jeremiah 1-7	2:4-12 5:1-9	2:13-35 3:20-21 6:16-19 7:21-29	3:19 6:9-10 7:2-7	3:12-15 3:22-25
God calls Jeremiah to prophesy about the return of God's people and about a new covenant God would make with them.	Jeremiah 29-33			29:10-11 31:16-20 31:31-34 33:14-26	29:12-14
Judah is conquered by Babylon, just as God's prophets had foretold.	Jeremiah 39-44, 52		40:2-3 42:13-17 43:1-7 44:1-30	42:9-12	39:15-18

Description	Bible Section	God is perfectly righteous, wise, and good	We are separated from God's goodness by our sin	God wants to bless us and reconcile with us	We reconcile with God when we trust his good news
This poem of lament affirms God's righteous judgment on Jerusalem and appeals to God for restoration.	Lamentations	1:18 2:17 3:37-39	1:5 1:8 1:14	3:21-23 3:31-33	3:24-26
Daniel is captured from Judah and sent into exile, but he trusts God even as he serves the reigning government.	Daniel 1-6	2:19-22 4:34-35 4:37			3:16-18 3:28-29
God calls Ezekiel to proclaim a message of repentance to Judah's exiles and to proclaim a promise of restoration to God's people.	Ezekiel 33-37	33:17-20 36:22-23	33:10 33:29	33:11 34:11-31 36:8-15 37:12-14	
Esther, a Jew in exile, is promoted to a position of influence. Esther then risks her life to save her Jewish people.	Esther			4:14 6:13 9:20-28 10:2-3	
God uses the reigning government to prompt the Jewish exiles to return to Jerusalem and rebuild the temple.	Ezra 1-6	3:10-11		1:1-7 6:6-14 6:22	
God calls Nehemiah to return to Jerusalem and lead the Jewish exiles to rebuild the city wall.	Nehemiah 1-6		1:4-11	2:4-8 2:17-18 6:15-16	

ON YOUR SIDE TODAY

Description	Bible Section	God is perfectly righteous, wise, and good	We are separated from God's goodness by our sin	God wants to bless us and reconcile with us	We reconcile with God when we trust his good news
God calls Zechariah to proclaim the return of God's people and prophesy about a special servant-king who would save them from their sins.	Zechariah		7:8-14	1:3-6 2:10-13 3:8-10 9:9-17	
God calls Malachi to urge God's people to stay faithful and to prophesy about a messenger who would announce the coming of the Lord.	Malachi	2:17 3:13-15	1:6-14 2:10-16	3:1-4 3:7-12	3:16-18 4:2-3
Jesus, the promised servant-king who would save God's people from their sins, is born to Mary and Joseph in Bethlehem.	Matthew 1:18-25			1:21-23	
John the Baptist, the promised messenger, preaches repentance and announces the coming of the Lord.	Matthew 3		3:5-6	3:1-3	
Nicodemus visits Jesus, and John the Baptist answers an objection about Jesus.	John 3	3:31-33	3:19-20	3:16-17	3:14-16 3:18
Jesus meets an outcast Samaritan woman who then shares the good news with her village.	John 4:1-42			4:10-14 4:31-36	4:39-42
Jesus goes up on a mountain and teaches many things about the kingdom of God.	Matthew 5-7	5:44-48 6:9-10	5:17-20 5:21-22 5:27-30 6:12-15	5:3-12 6:11 6:25-34 7:7-11	

Description	Bible Section	God is perfectly righteous, wise, and good	We are separated from God's goodness by our sin	God wants to bless us and reconcile with us	We reconcile with God when we trust his good news
Jesus heals a paralyzed man next to a pool, and he teaches that God his Father sent him to bring eternal life.	John 5	5:17-23 5:25-30		5:6-14	5:24 5:37-40
Jesus heals a paralyzed man who is lowered to him on a stretcher, and he teaches that he is able and willing to forgive sinners.	Mark 2:1-17			2:3-5 2:10-12 2:14-17	2:5
Jesus is anointed by a sinful woman at a meal, and he teaches about the nature of forgiveness and gratefulness.	Luke 7:36-50			7:40-48	7:50
Jesus teaches about how the word of God spreads, and he calms a stormy sea.	Mark 4:1-40			4:24-32 4:38-41	4:20
Jesus teaches that he is the good shepherd who lays down his life for his sheep.	John 10	10:29-38		10:2-18	10:24-28
Jesus teaches that the real treasure is found in God and in God's kingdom.	Luke 12:13-34			12:22-34	
Jesus teaches about how God pursues lost people and that he celebrates when they are found.	Luke 15			15:4-7 15:8-10 15:17-24	

Description	Bible Section	God is perfectly righteous, wise, and good	We are separated from God's goodness by our sin	God wants to bless us and reconcile with us	We reconcile with God when we trust his good news
Jesus teaches about greatness, sin, and forgiveness.	Matthew 18		18:6-9	18:10-14 18:21-35	
Jesus teaches about prayer and humility, and blesses little children brought to him.	Luke 18:1-17		18:9-14	18:6-8 18:15-17	18:13-14
Jesus spots Zaccheus in a tree and goes to his house for dinner.	Luke 19:1-10			19:5-7 19:9-10	
Jesus teaches that God wants to be generous to all kinds of followers.	Matthew 20:1-16	20:8-16		20:1-7	
Jesus raises Lazarus from the dead.	John 11	11:4		11:5 11:14-15 11:41-44	11:25-27
Jesus foretells his death, spends a last Passover with his disciples, and establishes the Lord's Supper.	Matthew 26:1-35			26:26-28	
Jesus teaches his disciples at the Last Supper.	John 14-16			14:16-27 15:9-17 16:7-15 16:20-22	14:1-7
Jesus prays at the Last Supper.	John 17	17:1-5		17:9-19 17:24-26	17:6-8 17:20-23
Jesus prays with great sorrow at Gethsemane. He is then betrayed, arrested, tried, and sentenced to die on a cross.	Matthew 26:36-27:26	26:39,42,44 26:52-56			

Description	Bible Section	God is perfectly righteous, wise, and good	We are separated from God's goodness by our sin	God wants to bless us and reconcile with us	We reconcile with God when we trust his good news
Jesus is crucified, dies, and is buried.	Luke 23:33-56	23:47	23:40-41	23:34 23:44-46	23:41-43
Jesus rises from the dead, appears to his disciples, and ascends back to the Father.	Luke 24			24:6-8 24:25-27 24:32 24:44-53	
Empowered by the Holy Spirit, the disciples proclaim the good news. Thousands of people believe in Jesus.	Acts 1-4	3:11-15 4:24-28		2:5-36 3:6-10 3:21-26	2:21 2:37-41 3:19-20 4:12
Saul, an enemy of the growing Jesus movement, believes in Jesus and begins sharing the good news.	Acts 9	9:13-16		9:10-12 9:17 9:36-41	9:18-22
God shows Peter that both Jews and Gentiles are included in the good news.	Acts 10	10:13-16 10:19-22 10:28-29 10:34-35		10:36-43	10:43-48
Saul becomes known as Paul and travels widely, sharing the good news.	Acts 13-28	17:24-31	13:46 19:9 28:25-27	13:16-37 14:15-17 18:9-10 26:1-23	13:38-41 13:47-48 15:7-18 16:30-34
Paul writes a letter to believers in Rome.	Romans	1:16-21 3:25-26 11:33-36 16:25-27	3:9-20 3:23 7:9-11	4:6-8 5:6-11 8:26-39	3:21-24,28 5:1-2 6:22-23 10:9-13
Paul writes a letter to believers in Corinth.	1 Corinthians		6:9-10 11:27-32	2:9-12 15:20-26 15:50-58	1:18-25 6:11 11:23-26 15:1-5
Paul writes another letter to believers in Corinth.	2 Corinthians			1:3-5 4:14-18 5:1-5 9:8-15	2:15-16 5:17-21 6:1-2

ON YOUR SIDE TODAY

Description	Bible Section	God is perfectly righteous, wise, and good	We are separated from God's goodness by our sin	God wants to bless us and reconcile with us	We reconcile with God when we trust his good news
Paul writes a letter to believers in Galatia.	Galatians	1:3-5	3:10-13	4:4-7	2:15-21 3:1-9 3:14-29
Paul writes a letter to believers in Ephesus.	Ephesians	1:3-6 1:17-19	2:1-3 5:5-7	1:7-10 2:4-5 2:13-17 3:14-19	1:11-14 2:4-10 2:18-22 5:8-10
Paul writes a letter to believers in Philippi.	Philippians	2:6-11		3:20-21 4:4-9 4:12-13 4:19	1:21-24 3:7-11
Paul writes a letter to believers in Colossae.	Colossians	1:15-20 2:9-10	1:21 3:5-7	1:22-23	1:3-6 1:13-14 1:22-23 2:11-14
Paul writes a letter to believers in Thessalonica.	1 Thessalonians	2:11-12		4:15-18	1:8-10 2:13 4:13-14 5:8-10
Paul writes another letter to believers in Thessalonica.	2 Thessalonians			2:16-17 3:3-5	1:3-10 2:13-14
Paul writes a letter to Timothy, a close friend and fellow church planter.	1 Timothy	1:17 6:15-16	1:15	2:3-6 6:17	4:10 6:11-12
Paul writes another letter to Timothy.	2 Timothy			1:7 3:14-17 4:18	1:8-12 2:10-13
Paul writes a letter to Titus, a fellow church planter.	Titus		3:3	2:11-14 3:4-5	3:6-8
Paul writes a letter to Philemon, a close friend.	Philemon			1:8-10	1:4-6 1:15-16

The Truly Good Book

Description	Bible Section	God is perfectly righteous, wise, and good	We are separated from God's goodness by our sin	God wants to bless us and reconcile with us	We reconcile with God when we trust his good news
A Christian leader writes a general letter to believers.	Hebrews	1:2-3 13:20-21	3:7-19	6:13-19 9:24-28 12:3-11 13:5-6	7:24-27 10:35-39 13:14-15
James writes a general letter to believers.	James	1:13	1:14-15 4:1-4	1:2-5 1:12 1:16-17 5:10-11	2:14-26
Peter writes a general letter to believers.	1 Peter	5:10-11		1:3-7 2:9-10 4:14-16,19 5:6-7	2:24-25
Peter writes another general letter to believers.	2 Peter	1:16-21		1:3-4 3:8-9	1:1-2
John writes a general letter to believers.	1 John		1:8,10	1:9 2:1-2 4:9-10	1:7 3:23-24 4:14-16 5:1-5,10-13
Jude writes a general letter to believers.	Jude	1:24-25	1:3-19	1:1-2 1:24-25	1:20-21
John writes of his visions of Jesus delivering a message for seven churches.	Revelation 1-3	1:4-6,8	2:4-5,14-16 2:20-23 3:1-3 3:15-18	2:7,10-11 2:17,26-29 3:5-6,12-13 3:19-22	
John writes of his visions of the end of the age and the eternal kingdom of Jesus Christ.	Revelation 4-22	4:8-11 5:11-14 7:9-12 15:2-4	18:4-8 21:8 22:15	5:1-10 7:15-17 21:1-5 21:9-22:7	7:13-14 19:6-10 21:6-7 22:12-17

ACKNOWLEDGMENTS

I am very thankful for those in my family who have encouraged and supported my writing in many ways over the years. I want to especially thank Emily, Seth, and Chelsea, who have patiently endured my times of absence (and my absent-minded moments) while I worked on this book.

I am also very grateful to the talented professionals who helped bring this book to print. This includes Stephanie Cross, my delightful editor, who made the message cleaner, clearer, and more impactful; Sarah Sperry, my graphic designer, who nailed the cover art and inside layout; Jennifer Siao, my proofreader, who provided an excellent final review; and author Brian Croft, who gave me valuable guidance on how to get this book published.

I deeply appreciate the members of churches of which I've been a part, for they have invested in me and allowed me to learn and serve alongside them. These churches include Vineville Baptist (Macon, GA), Prince Avenue Baptist (Athens, GA), New Hope Baptist (Nicholson, GA), Metairie Baptist (Metairie, LA), First Baptist Sweetwater (Sweetwater, TN), and Hurstbourne Baptist (Louisville, KY).

Most of all, I am thankful to the God who made me, saved me, and dwells in me. Anything truly admirable in me is his handiwork. All glory goes to the Lord.

SOURCES

Chapter 1: Blindness
» (p. 1, English proverb) Thomas Fuller and Allan Ramsay, *Aphorisms of Wisdom; or, a Complete Collection of the Most Celebrated Proverbs, in the English, Scotch, French, Spanish, Italian, and Other Languages; Ancient and Modern, Collected and Digested. to Which Is Added, Ramsay's Collection of Scottish Proverbs* (Glasgow: R. Chapman, Trongate, for R. & D. Malcolm, 1814), 2.

Chapter 2: Motives
» (p. 10) Martin Luther, *Luther's Large Catechism: God's Call to Repentance, Faith and Prayer; the Bible Plan of Salvation Explained,* trans. John Nicholas Lenker (Minneapolis: Luther Press, 1908), 44.
» (p. 15, Katherine Anne Porter) George Plimpton, compiler, *Writers at Work: The Paris Review Interviews, Second Series* (New York: Viking Press, 1963), 161.
» (p. 23, Lord Byron) George Gordon, *Lord Byron: Selected Letters and Journals,* ed. Leslie A. Marchand (Cambridge: Belknap Press of Harvard University Press, 1982), 70.

Chapter 3: Wrath
» (p. 25) Miguel de Cervantes, *The Ingenious Gentleman Don Quixote of La Mancha, Volume II.* Translation with introduction by John Ormsby (New York: Century Co., 1907), 275, 513.
» (p. 31, Publilius Syrus) J. Wight Duff and Arnold M. Duff, trans., *Minor Latin Poets* (Cambridge, MA: Harvard University Press, 1935), 52-53.

Chapter 4: Sacrifice
» (p. 33, Unknown) This quote has been attributed, in various forms, to Robert Louis Stevenson, Amy Carmichael, and Victor Hugo, among others; but evidence for a primary source is lacking. An early variant appears in an article

by Rev. Harry Jones, "Essays on Texts: Charity," *The Leisure Hour* (London: Paternaster Row), January 1, 1870, 12. A closer version appears in an article by Rev. J.S. Maver, "Sermonettes on the Golden Texts," *The Expository Times, Vol. 10* (Edinburgh, T. & T, Clark), Oct 1898-Sept 1899, 183.

Chapter 5: Faith
» (p. 41) Brother Lawrence, *The Practice of the Presence of God.* Hendrickson Christian Classics (Peabody, Massachusetts: Hendrickson Publishers, 2004), 19.
» (p. 49) Blaise Pascal, *Pensées,* trans. A. J. Krailsheimer (New York: Penguin Books, 1995), 50.

Chapter 6: Happiness
» (p. 51) Ralph Hudson, "At the Cross" (refrain), *Baptist Hymnal* (Nashville: Convention Press, 1991), Hymn #139.
» (p. 54) Billy Graham, *The Secret of Happiness* (Dallas: Word Publishing, 1985), 6.
» (p. 55, Merriam-Webster Dictionary) "Joy," Merriam-Webster, accessed February 9, 2022, https://www.merriam-webster.com/dictionary/joy, and "Happiness," Merriam-Webster, accessed February 9, 2022, https://www.merriam-webster.com/dictionary/happiness.
» (p. 64) Mary Gardiner Brainard, "Not Knowing," in *An American Anthology: 1787-1900: Selections Illustrating the Editor's Critical Review of American Poetry in the Nineteenth Century,* ed. Edmund Clarence Stedman (New York: Houghton, Mifflin, and Company, 1900), 469-470.

Chapter 7: Forever
» (p. 71) C.S. Lewis, *Mere Christianity.* (Westwood, New Jersey: Barbour and Company/Macmillian Publishing, 1952), 115.

Appendix A: What I Did and Did Not Say
» (p. 87, E.B. White) William Strunk Jr., *The Elements of Style: with Revisions, an Introduction, and a Chapter on Writing by E.B. White, fourth edition* (Boston: Allyn and Bacon, 2000), 79.

Appendix B: The Truly Good Book
» (p. 91, Abraham Lincoln) Roy P. Basler, editor, *The Collected Works of Abraham Lincoln, Volume VII.* Abraham Lincoln Association, Springfield, Illinois (New Brunswick, New Jersey: Rutgers University Press, 1953), 542.

ABOUT THE AUTHOR

Jeffrey Michael Smith has been teaching the Bible and leading church ministries for most of his adult life. He has worked in full-time vocational ministry for over sixteen years. Since 2007, he has served on staff at Hurstbourne Baptist Church in Louisville, Kentucky, where he currently serves as their Administration and Discipleship Pastor.

Jeff has earned a bachelor of arts degree from the University of Georgia and a master of divinity degree from New Orleans Baptist Theological Seminary. He has taught courses on Bible teaching and Christian education ministry for Campbellsville University and trained Sunday School and Bible study leaders for the Kentucky Baptist Convention.

Jeff lives in Louisville, Kentucky. He enjoys reading, writing, running, and hanging out with his wife, Emily, and their two kids, Seth and Chelsea. Jeff blogs about the Bible and the good news of Jesus Christ at *onyoursidetoday.com*.

Made in the USA
Monee, IL
07 December 2023